Why Does Software Cost So Much?
And Other Puzzles
of the Information Age

Best Regards,

Tom DeMarco

WHY DOES SOFTWARE COST SO MUCH?
AND OTHER PUZZLES
OF THE INFORMATION AGE

BY
TOM DEMARCO

DORSET HOUSE PUBLISHING
353 WEST 12TH STREET
NEW YORK, NEW YORK 10014

Library of Congress Cataloging-in-Publication Data

DeMarco, Tom.
    Why does software cost so much? : and other puzzles of the
Information Age / by Tom DeMarco.
      p.   cm.
    Includes bibliographical references and index.
    ISBN 0-932633-34-X (pbk.)
    1. Computer software. 2. Software engineering. I. Title.
QA76.754.D42   1995
005.3--dc20   95-35656
                                                        CIP

Trademark credits: Apple®, Macintosh®, Open Look®, PowerBook®, and QuickTime® are registered trademarks of Apple Computer, Inc. CompuServe® is a registered trademark of CompuServe, Inc. CPM® is a registered trademark of Digital Research. Microsoft® and MS-DOS® are registered trademarks, and Windows™ is a trademark of Microsoft Corp. IBM®, OS/2®, PC®, PC/XT®, and PS/2® are registered trademarks and PowerPC™ is a trademark of International Business Machines Corp. NeXT® is a registered trademark of NeXT. PageMaker® is a registered trademark of Aldus Corp. Quicken® is a registered trademark of Intuit, Inc. SADT® is a registered trademark of SofTech, Inc. Unix® is a registered trademark of Unix Systems Labs. Mountain Dew®, Nerf®, and other trade or product names are either trademarks or registered trademarks of their respective companies, and are the property of their respective holders and should be treated as such.

Cover Illustration: Tom DeMarco
Cover Design: Jeff Faville, Faville Design

Distributed in the United Kingdom, Ireland, Europe, and Africa by John Wiley & Sons, Ltd., Chichester, Sussex, England. Distributed in the English language in Singapore, the Philippines, and southeast Asia by Toppan Co., Ltd., Singapore; and in the English language in Japan by Toppan Co., Ltd., Tokyo, Japan.

Printed in the United States of America

Library of Congress Catalog Number 95-35656

ISBN: 0-932633-34-X   12 11 10 9 8 7 6 5 4 3 2 1

ACKNOWLEDGMENTS

We gratefully acknowledge the following organizations for permission to reprint these selected articles in this volume:

[1] "Why Does Software Cost So Much?" Copyright ® 1993 IEEE. Reprinted, with permission, from *IEEE Software,* March 1993.

[3] "Management-Aided Software Engineering," with Sheila Brady. Copyright ® 1994 IEEE. Reprinted, with permission, from *IEEE Software,* November 1994.

[5] "Standing Naked in the Snow (Variation on a Theme by Yamaura)" originally appeared in the monthly journal *American Programmer,* December 1994. Copyright ® 1994. Reprinted, with permission, from Cutter Information Corp., Arlington, MA 02174 (tel 617/648-8702, fax 617/648-1950).

[7] "Desktop Video: A Tutorial." Copyright ® 1991. Reprinted, with permission of the Boston Computer Society, from *The Active Window,* March 1991.

[8] "Nontechnological Issues in Software Engineering." Copyright ® 1991 IEEE. Reprinted, with permission, from the *Proceedings of the 13th International Conference on Software Engineering.* Austin, Tex., 1991.

[9] "Challenge of the '90s: The Schools." Copyright ® 1990 IEEE. Reprinted, with permission, from *IEEE Software,* November 1990.

[10] "Software Development: State of the Art vs. State of the Practice," with Tim Lister. Copyright ® 1989 ACM. Reprinted, with permission, from the *Proceedings of the 11th International Conference on Software Engineering.* Pittsburgh, 1989.

[11] "Software Productivity: The Covert Agenda." Reprinted from *Deadline*, May 1988.

[14] "Icons" originally appeared in the monthly journal *American Programmer*, April 1992. Copyright © 1992. Reprinted, with permission, from Cutter Information Corp., Arlington, MA 02174 (tel 617/648-8702, fax 617/648-1950).

[16] "Use of Video for Program Documentation," with Curt Geertgens. Copyright © 1990 IEEE. Reprinted, with permission, from the *Proceedings of the 12th International Conference on Software Engineering*. Nice, France, 1990.

[17] "Structured Analysis: The Beginnings of a New Discipline." Reprinted from *Deadline*, December 1989.

[18] "The First Pastist Pronouncement" originally appeared in the monthly journal *American Programmer*, August 1988. Copyright © 1988. Reprinted, with permission, from Cutter Information Corp., Arlington, MA 02174 (tel 617/648-8702, fax 617/648-1950).

[19] "The Second Pastist Pronouncement" originally appeared in the monthly journal *American Programmer*, March 1989. Copyright © 1989. Reprinted, with permission, from Cutter Information Corp., Arlington, MA 02174 (tel 617/648-8702, fax 617/648-1950).

[20] "Twenty Years of Software Engineering: Looking Forward, Looking Back." Copyright © 1989 ACM. Reprinted, with permission, from the *Proceedings of the 11th International Conference on Software Engineering*. Pittsburgh, 1989.

CONTENTS

PREFACE

ABSTRACTION AND INSIGHT

An *abstraction* is a pattern that fits, and to some extent explains, phenomena that would otherwise appear unrelated. An *insight* is a particularly useful abstraction, one that you happen not to have come upon before. When you encounter an insight, something inside you prompts a fundamentally human response: You say, "Aha!" and you feel good all over. Sometimes, you laugh.

This built-in reward system for insight is part of Evolution's grand strategy for humans. She wants us to seek good, new abstractions and treasure them when we find them. She wants us to be learners. In this way, she is trying to make us into abstraction engines and, with her ingenious insight-reward system, she is doing a pretty good job of it.

Insight, as I have defined it, is the essential ingredient of any good essay. May the ones that follow bring you some of this wonderful rare commodity. I hope they make you go Aha! from time to time, and maybe even laugh.

June 1995   T.D.M.
Camden, Maine

1

WHY DOES SOFTWARE COST SO MUCH?

Judging by the number of requests to reprint this first essay and the controversy it stirred up, I've concluded "Why Does Software Cost So Much?" is the most successful piece I've ever written. All the hullabaloo took me somewhat by surprise. The premise of the essay is one that I feel deeply about, but I always figured that was just something weird about me. Now I'm beginning to suspect that it's something weird about *us*, the members of the software community. Every time we're lectured about the outrageous cost of software, we tend to think about all the wonders software has created. We tend to indulge ourselves in that not-politically-correct thought: Maybe transforming the world ought not to come too cheap. . . .

1

WHY DOES SOFTWARE COST SO MUCH?

In the absence of meaningful standards, a new industry like software comes to depend instead on *folklore*. As the industry matures, a first order of business is to recognize and question the folklore. I propose to do this by considering that familiar question: "Why does software cost so much?" How we ask that question and how we answer it reveal much about our folklore.

WHEN DID YOU STOP BEATING YOUR WIFE?

Author and consultant Jerry Weinberg [1] claims to have encountered the question "Why does software cost so much?" more than any other in his long career. The correct answer, he says, is "Compared to what?" There is a likable logic to that: Most of the things we do with software in the 1990s are barely conceivable without software, so there is no valid basis of comparison. Yet Jerry's answer, charming as it may be, won't do you much good. At best, it will just annoy your questioner. No answer is going to satisfy the questioner (typically your boss or user), because he or she *is not really interested in an answer*. People don't ask that question to have an answer.

"Why does software cost so much?" is not a question at all; it's an assertion. The assertion is that software is too pricey. The person who poses this rhetorical question may seem to be motivated by mere intellectual curiosity: "Gee, I've always wondered, just why is it that software costs so much?" The real motivation, however, has nothing to do with curiosity. It has only to do with getting the brutal assertion on the table. It's a negotiating position. You are being put on notice that software costs unconscionably much to build, and no budget or schedule you're likely to request will be considered reasonable. Your boss or user may agree to your budget, but only under *extreme* duress. Since the amount budgeted is already terribly, terribly excessive, any slip or overrun is virtually a crime against nature.

In a recent interview [2], Cadre Technologies founder Lou Mazzucchelli observes that "software consumers are not satisfied with either the quantity or the quality of our output." Right on target. Software consumers in vast numbers are telling us that our efforts just don't begin to measure up to their expectations. Software, at least the kind that companies build for their own use, is much too expensive, takes too long to build, isn't robust enough, and isn't easy enough to use or good enough in any other way either.

Now I have a very grumpy question for those who complain that the software development community hasn't measured up to their expectations: Where in hell did those expectations come from?

WE INTERRUPT THIS SOBER TREATISE FOR A DIATRIBE

You and I and others like us built the software industry from scratch over the last thirty years. We started with thin air and made it into a $300 billion a year business. (See [3] to understand how I arrive at this figure.) In all of economic history, there has never been a more staggering accomplishment. Think of that. In the time it takes for you to read this article, the software industry will have generated something more than $12 million.

What has it taken to build this huge new industry so quickly? Hint: It wasn't just getting some programmers together and teaching them to sling code. It required the active participation of a marketplace. Somebody had to toady up huge quantities of money to buy all the software we built. And they did. Not only did a lot of somebodies buy all we could produce at the cost we charged, they complained about not being able to buy even more, about the so-called software backlog.

All of this growth was not the result of poor quality and poor productivity. The only conceivable explanation for the phenomenal success of the software industry is that it has regularly delivered a standard of quality and productivity far beyond the real expectations of the market. But all the time that our buyers (our managers and our users) were lining up to cash in on the bargain, they were complaining. Their actions and their words gave two diametrically opposed messages.

Before I comment on why this might be, it's interesting to observe that this isn't a recent phenomenon. They didn't congratulate us for years and years and then only become upset at the downturn in the 1990s. No, they complained all the way from zero to $300 billion a year.

I myself am a bit peeved by this. (Perhaps you could tell.) I feel like we have accomplished wonders and been yelled at the whole time.

AN ANALOGY FROM 1904

Imagine how the Wright brothers would have felt had they had a similar reception. Imagine you're Orville, for example. It's December 7, 1904, at Kitty Hawk, North Carolina, 7:30 A.M., and you're clambering into Flyer One. "Let 'er rip," you say, or words to that effect. The engine coughs to life. You rev it up and there's movement. There is not just movement, there is speed, speed and bumps and wind and . . . by God, you're up! You're off the ground. This is it: heavier-than-air flight! You've done it. You've pulled off a miracle, and the world will never be the same. You're so elated you're barely even afraid. Like a practiced pilot, you bring the flyer down.

But just as you're coming to a stop, you notice a guy in a business suit, holding an attaché case and looking sourly at his watch. He approaches and says, "Orville, I'm really disappointed in this project. I had great expectations of you and you've let me down. Here it is, nearly 8 A.M., and I have to be in L.A. for a dinner meeting tonight. And you guys are nowhere! You haven't invented the jet engine yet or the stewardess or the airport or airline meals or those little drinks in miniature bottles. You've let me down completely! I'm going to miss my meeting and it's all your fault."

That guy in the suit is the software consumer whom Lou Mazzuchelli was talking about, the user or manager who is "not satisfied with either the quantity or the quality of our output."

NOW THE TRUTH ABOUT WHERE
THOSE EXPECTATIONS COME FROM

No one ever expected the software industry to achieve what it has achieved. Not a single futurist predicted the extraordinary productivity and quality we have accomplished. Then how is it possible that the industry as a whole is performing beyond the wildest expectations, while all the individual projects are under-performing outrageously? It's not possible. Those projects aren't underperforming at all, and their consumers know it. Pay attention to what they do, not what they say, to get the real message. The real message is that software consumers are telling us our software is the best bargain they ever heard of.

So why all the bellyaching? People complain to us *because they know we work harder when they complain.* We have trained them to do this. When they complained in the past, we worked harder. We gave them more for their money (even more than the extraordinary bargain they would have gotten anyway) because they pretended to be discontented. Boy, are we dumb.

A HELPFUL HINT FROM THE ACADEMIC COMMUNITY

In a recent article [4], authors Professors Lederer and Prasad set down some guidelines for better software cost estimating and perhaps unintentionally provided some insight about managerial complaints that software costs too much. Their guidelines were derived from a survey on estimating techniques mailed to a sample of some four hundred professional software managers. What seemed more important to me than any of the article's conclusions was a tiny "factoid" tucked away in their commentary about the survey responses: The great majority of respondents reported that their software estimates were dismal ("only about one in four projects is completed at a cost reasonably close to the estimate"), but they weren't on the whole dissatisfied with the estimating process. Lederer and Prasad report that

> *forty-three percent of the subjects indicated that their current estimating was "very satisfactory" or "moderately satisfactory" (the two highest ratings).*

What's going on here? Software estimates bear little or no resemblance to reality, but the managers aren't dissatisfied? How can that be? Oh . . . I think I'm beginning to understand. Maybe the purpose of the estimating process is not to come up with a realistic answer, but to come up with an *unrealistic* answer. Maybe the estimating process is not supposed to guide managers as to what to expect. Rather, it's supposed to guide them as to what to *pretend* to expect. This is the kind of estimating process that tells your boss, for example, to set September 1995 as the "right" expected delivery date for your new project. It provides a schedule that is neither ridiculous nor feasible. That is, after all, the object of the exercise. It is the very definition of the "right" schedule:

> The right schedule is one that is *utterly* impossible, just not *obviously* impossible.

HOW DO MANAGERS KNOW?

It is a great tribute to quality software management that managers know unerringly how to set this right schedule. This task isn't easy. In the abstract, at least, it is just as hard to predict a date that is just short of possible as to pick one that is safe and reasonable. Both require some prediction of what the true achievement capability of a team will be, and that is a difficult matter.

How do our managers learn to do this hard thing? Again, the answer is we've trained them. They watch our faces when they set schedules. If we look relieved, they know they haven't turned the screws enough. If we just giggle at them, they know they've gone too far.

SUCCESS IN ESTIMATING AND FAILURE IN BUSINESS

"Why does software cost so much?" is an assertion masquerading as a question. The assertion that software is too expensive is part of a cost-containment ploy. The cynical notion that a good schedule is one that no one has a prayer of achieving is another part of that ploy. The constant refrain that software developers just are not productive enough has only one purpose: to make software developers work harder. It is a goad, a goad that appears to work because software developers are sincere and professional and a little dopey.

The problem is our industry is over-goaded. The work of software development is largely incompressible. When you're under pressure, your first response is to cut out extraneous activities: chats and bull sessions. That may indeed be productive, but as the pressure continues, there is nothing more you can do. You can't work faster; you might stay later, but that has a long-term cost in your personal life. A little overtime in the next week may help to achieve Friday's deadline, but overtime applied over months and months gives only an illusion of progress. The apparent progress of overtime is wiped out by compensatory "under-time," burnout, disillusionment, waste, and employee turnover.

As the pressure increases, the only real option is to pay for speed by reducing quality. I sometimes think, rather bitterly, that reduced quality is a conscious goal of those who pressure projects. They are saying, "Loosen up, folks. Learn to rush the product out the door without worrying so much about quality." This comes, of course, at the very moment that companies are paying lip service to quality as never before.

In the short term, paying for speed by reducing quality seems to make sense. It wins us a few battles, but never the war. In the long run, that compromise will take us just where it took the American automobile industry in the 1980s: to reduced prominence in the market and reduced capacity to compete with new global players.

THE MORAL

If you ask the wrong question, you'll never get the right answer. Instead of asking "Why does software cost so much?" we need to begin asking "What have we done to make it possible for today's software to cost so little?" The answer to that question will help us continue the extraordinary level of achievement that has always distinguished the software industry.

REFERENCES

[1] Gerald M. Weinberg, *Quality Software Management, Vol. 1: Systems Thinking* (New York: Dorset House Publishing, 1992).

[2] "Lou Mazzucchelli on Software Engineering," *Computer Design,* August 1991, pp. 25-27.

[3] John E. Hopcroft and Dean B. Krafft, "Toward Better Computer Science," *IEEE Spectrum,* Vol. 24, No. 12 (December 1987), pp. 58-60.

[4] A.L. Lederer and J. Prasad, "Nine Management Guidelines for Better Cost Estimating," Communications of the ACM, Vol. 35, No. 2 (February 1992), pp. 51-59.

2

MAD ABOUT MEASUREMENT

This essay is adapted from a keynote address I gave to the 5th International Conference on Applications of Software Measurement in La Jolla, Calif., November 9, 1994. The audience that day was large and warm, and much of the presentation was born on the stage, child of the magic that sometimes happens with a great audience.

2

MAD ABOUT MEASUREMENT

Not previously published.

Having worked during much of the last decade and a half in the area of software metrics, I find myself more and more troubled by the role of this now prominent component of our industry. The title I have chosen for this essay is meant to betray some of my ambivalence on the subject. The title can be read in two opposite ways, leaving one to wonder, Is the author madly positive about the success of software measurement? or Is he positively mad that our measurement hasn't really paid off? The answer is yes, I am. Both.

Any book you pick up on the subject of software metrics (my own *Controlling Software Projects* [1] included) is likely to be in the madly positive category. There is a mantra that runs through these books, something along the lines of "Look, here is *yet another* wonderful metric that could show you useful things about how your organization or project is doing." Many of the metrics are indeed compelling. The aggregate message, however, is what has begun to bother me. That message is

> Metrics Are Good.
> More Would Be Better.
> Most Is Best.

Though never stated in so many words, this message is everywhere. It is at the heart of metrics books, conferences, seminars, and articles. You can hardly focus on the literally hundreds of metrics proposed by Basili, Boehm, DeMarco and Lister, Gilb, Grady and Caswell, Jones, Matsubara, McCabe, Putnam, Rubin, and others without wondering uneasily if you really oughtn't to be collecting *all* of them. God, no.

This may seem obvious, but somebody really ought to say it: Metrics cost a ton of money. It costs a lot to collect them badly and a lot more to collect them well.

How much is enough?

In early 1984, my colleague Tim Lister and I visited what was then one of America's premier computer makers. We lectured and consulted there for a week. One of the things we noticed immediately was a culture of interruption in the software group. That meant developers could rarely work for more than a few minutes at a time on any one task. To call their attention to this, we suggested they begin to measure the length of work periods, uninterrupted chunks of time in which the developer could work obsessively on one thing and one thing only. This would involve some bookkeeping about each interruption, but it would have the positive effect of focusing attention on the value of extended chunks, and the frustration caused by the interruptions. The company agreed.

Years later, I called a contact in the company on another matter and was astounded to learn that they were still tracking interrupts. The rate had stabilized within a few months and all the value of building interrupt awareness had long since been realized. But they were still writing down the time and the cause of each interrupt.

I am sorry to say that that once great company is now not nearly so great. I do hope that Tim Lister and I were not the direct cause.

Since I have been as guilty as anyone in overselling the idea of software metrics, it is perhaps incumbent on me to set the record straight on just how much metrics data collection makes sense. Here is my best shot at it:

> **DeMarco's Mea Culpa Premise**
>
> I can only think of one metric that is worth collecting now and forever: defect count. Any organization that fails to track and type defects is running at less than its optimal level.
>
> There are many other metrics that are worth collecting *for a while.* Each time you introduce and begin collecting a new metric, you need to put in place a mechanism to cease collecting that metric at some time in the future.
>
> Many of the most useful metrics should be collected only on a sampling basis.

MEASUREMENT: AT ITS BEST AND AT ITS WORST

Sure, measurement costs money, but it does have the potential to help us work more effectively. At its best, the use of software metrics can inform and guide developers, and help organizations to improve. At its worst, it can do actual harm. And there is an entire range between the two extremes, varying all the way from function to dysfunction. It may be useful to bound this range with an example from each extreme.

First, the positive: Metrics could be defined as the discipline of counting things and observing and profiting from patterns found among the things we count. That is also a pretty fair definition of *science.* My sense of what science is has been affected over this last year by a new friendship with the biologist Uldis Roze, author of *The North American Porcupine* [2]. Much of what we know about porcupines today, about their habits and habitat, comes from painstaking (and often painful) research performed by Uldis Roze. You can't listen for long to the man describe his work without becoming aware of the central role of counting in porcupine research. He counts quills under trees to guess how much time the animals spend in each type of tree. He counts populations, numbers in their litters, death rates due to various kinds of injury and illness, droppings, bone fractures, quill density in various parts of the body . . . anything that will hold still, he counts it.

Over dinner one night with our families, Uldis told a story to make that very point: He told of a little girl, ten years old, who had shown a budding interest in science. Her father, also a biologist, wondered what he could do to encourage her interest. Since her birthday was coming up, he thought about what kind of a gift would be right: a microscope, perhaps? or a chemistry set? But those seemed far too glitzy for his notion of what real science was. Finally, he hit upon the idea of giving her a click-counter. He set her to work in the nearby woods, counting anything she wanted to discover what she could about the natural world.

That image has stayed with me ever since, a symbol of the practice of science (and of metrics) at its best. I offer it as a guidepost to mark one end of the function/dysfunction spectrum: a little girl in the forest, bent on discovery, with a click-counter in her hand.

As an example of metrics at their worst, consider the case of the Soviet nail factory that was measured on the basis of the number of nails produced. The factory managers hit upon the idea of converting their entire factory to production of only the smallest nails, tiny brads. Some commissar, realizing this as a case of dysfunction, came up with a remedy. He instituted measurement of *tonnage* of nails produced, rather than numbers. The factory immediately switched over to producing only railroad spikes. The image I propose to mark the dysfunction end of the spectrum is a Soviet carpenter, looking perplexed, with a useless brad in one hand and an equally useless railroad spike in the other.

Now where does your organization stand along this spectrum? Are you closer to the little girl with the click-counter, or closer to the carpenter staring in puzzlement at the two useless nails? Are you closer to function or dysfunction? Don't be too quick to answer. Dysfunction is far more common than you may think.

To help you place yourself and your organization, you need to understand why you collect metrics in the first place. I observe there are at least three different reasons we collect metrics, as follows:

1. to discover facts about our world
2. to steer our actions
3. to modify human behavior

We might arrange these, too, in a spectrum:

Behavior Modification —— Steering —— Discovery

Though I haven't yet given a formal definition of what I mean by *dysfunction,* I think you can sense that it is toward the left side of this spectrum where dysfunction is most likely to occur, and toward the right side where dysfunction is least likely; we may err in our attempts to discover, but we are not prone to systemic dysfunction. The middle ground, Steering, lies between the extremes in its propensity toward dysfunction.

Where does the discipline of software metrics lie on this spectrum? Well, we certainly started off, in the 1970s, to measure in order to discover. Indeed, we begin most presentations on measurement with some appropriate paean to Discovery. For instance, the following quote crops up in the first chapter or two of most measurement books:

> When you can measure what you are speaking about, and express it in numbers, you know something about it; but when you cannot measure it, when you cannot express it in numbers, your knowledge is of a meager and unsatisfactory kind: it may be the beginning of knowledge, but you have scarcely, in your thoughts, advanced to the stage of science. [Lord Kelvin, 1891]

In other words, Lord Kelvin suggests that we measure to know. My own quote "You can't control what you can't measure" implies that we measure to steer. But I'm beginning to wonder.

When we measure productivity, for example, we don't really do it to discover what our productivity is or to steer ourselves consistent with our actual productive capacity. When we measure productivity, we are stating loud and clear that we want productivity to increase. It's a goad. Similarly, when we measure defects, we are stating that we want the number of defects to be reduced. Neither of these statements is a bad goal in itself. But the measurements that lead toward them are neither Discovery nor Steering metrics. They are squarely in the camp of Behavior Modification, which leads me to the first of what will eventually become five Disquieting Thoughts About Software Metrics:

DT#1:	Have we practitioners of software metrics little by little gotten out of the Discovery and Steering business and into the Behavior Modification business?

If so, we are increasingly exposed to the possibility of dysfunction, of unwittingly causing outcomes that are squarely at odds with our goals.

A WORD OR TWO ABOUT NONMEASUREMENT

Measurement programs, from the simplest to the most elaborate, all have the same goal: to make the organization more effective. But can we really say, after all these years of focusing on measurement, that organizations that do measure their software processes are on the whole more efficient than those that don't? There are a few impressive counterexamples, Microsoft and Apple to name just two companies, that make no systematic use of software measurement. During the last decade, a period of triumphant ascendancy of software metrics as a discipline, these two companies have done just fine without. They aren't the only ones either. The entire small-cap sector is not known for its measurement practices, yet the solid vitality of the American economy since 1980 has come almost entirely from these small companies.

Compare two organizations known respectively for measurement and nonmeasurement: IBM and Microsoft. What we see is that a propensity toward lots of software measurement at IBM is part of a larger pattern of activities that are prominent there and that have almost no counterpart at Microsoft: IBM is keen on the Software Engineering Institute's Capability Maturity Model (CMM), and Microsoft isn't. IBM has "fat book" methodologies, and Microsoft doesn't. IBM generates an enormous quantity of documentation as part of its software lifecycle, and Microsoft generates almost none. IBM is dedicated to ISO-9000 compliance and certification and Microsoft has simply thumbed its nose at ISO-9000.

What do the SEI's model, elaborate methodologies, copious documentation, and ISO-9000 compliance all have in common? Together, they can be interpreted as signs of *institutionalization.* Organizations characterized by all of these factors are the ones we tend to call "institutions," and the organizations that practice none of the above are something else. IBM is an institution, and Microsoft is a very large economic organism trying its best not to be an institution.

Considering software metrics in light of this pattern leads to my second Disquieting Thought About Software Metrics:

DT#2:   Is all of our measurement effort just part of a trend toward institutionalization?

I suspect there is at least some truth to that grim conjecture. Certainly, the companies best represented at metrics conferences and tutorials tend to be the most institutional ones. If that's true, it's bad news. I never wanted to be part of the institutionalization of anything, and I suspect you didn't either.

MEASUREMENT DYSFUNCTION

In this section, I present three brief examples of measurement dysfunction and, finally, a definition. My intention here is first to show you some of the patterns of dysfunction, and second to impress upon you that dysfunction is more prevalent than we like to acknowledge; dysfunction is not the exception to the rule, but the rule itself [3]. Two of the examples come from software measurement and one from outside our field.

Hitachi

The first example is taken from Hitachi Software. The dysfunction detected there is particularly depressing as it happened in the context of an altogether admirable bit of good science and good discovery measurement conducted by Hitachi's then Chief Scientist, Tomoo Matsubara. In the late 1970s, Matsubara had begun to suspect that early detected defects could be a positive indication of as-yet-undetected defects. This relationship works particularly well if applied at a well-defined project checkpoint, say, end of unit test. The more defects you'd already found in your module through unit testing, according to Matsubara's rule, the more there were still to be found. Although counterintuitive, we now know this to be true in general and a powerful tool for assessing quality of a partly debugged product. It provides a reliable prediction of what Matsubara calls "latent defects." [4]

Hitachi moved quickly to exploit this relationship by tracking defects detected during the early testing, predicting latent defects still in the product, and then tracking the late integration testing process by comparing defects detected against latent defects suspected to be still in the code. This technique enabled them to produce a "quality-progress diagram," which they used to predict progress toward acceptable quality and to control project endgame activities (see Fig. 1).

No dysfunction yet. The scheme proved workable on a number of projects and eventually became integral to Hitachi's measurement program.

In March 1989, I received an astonishing letter from a young friend who was working under Matsubara at Hitachi. He reported that they had begun to detect a most curious misuse of

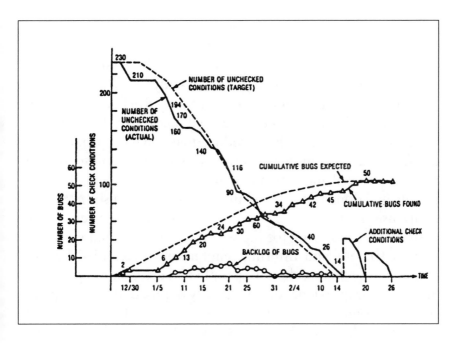

Figure I. Hitachi's quality-progress diagram.

the latent defect mechanism. Programmers had come to understand that more defects shown during unit test caused management to predict still more yet to be found. That translated to pressure on those workers to find an expected number of latent defects as the project neared its ship date. Consciously or unconsciously, developers began holding back defects found during unit test. Holding back a defect benefits the individual developers in three ways: They look good at the end of unit test, since their modules appear relatively defect free; they have fewer latent defects ascribed to their code, hence less pressure later; and they have one or two defects ready to produce during integration testing when management clamors for more: "Here's a defect I just found, Boss," they say, artfully neglecting to mention that they just found it in a pocket. Holding back defects benefits the developer, but doesn't benefit the organization at all. It is a clear example of dysfunction.

Sears

My second example of dysfunction is from outside the software field. You probably have already heard about it: the 1992 confession by marketing giant Sears, Roebuck & Co. that the company "may have acted against its customers' best interests" in selling them unneeded product maintenance programs. In brief, the sales commission structure had given salespeople an incentive to sell more maintenance agreements, and the salespeople had done just that, selling far more than customers could really use. In June 1992, Sears addressed an open letter to its customers apologizing for the way the incentives had worked to their detriment and offering reimbursement. Guided by their commission scheme, the salespeople had acted in a way that, as Sears later acknowledged, was directly opposed to the company's real goals—another example of measurement dysfunction at work.

About the time of the Sears fiasco, I happened to be returning a pair of ski gauntlets to L.L. Bean in Freeport, Maine. The gauntlets had begun to come apart at a seam. I have an old engineer's bias that seams should be stronger than the material they join, and so I was unsatisfied. But I was also a bit sheepish. After all, these gloves had served me well for two whole seasons. I explained the problem to the customer service agent, including my feeling about the required integrity of seams. And then I asked her if I was being unreasonable. "What do you think?" I asked. She looked down at my sales slip to catch my name. "Mr. DeMarco, it doesn't matter what I think. It only matters what *you* think, and you think the seam ought to be stronger than the fabric. So we're going to take these gauntlets back and give you a new pair or your money back, and we're going to tell the makers to strengthen their seams."

What was L.L. Bean doing that Sears had neglected? Somehow, L.L. Bean had caused this young employee to put herself in founder Leon L. Bean's shoes, to ask herself, "How would Mr. Bean handle this customer? How would he want me to act?" Sears instead had its salesfolk asking themselves, "How does the commission plan want me to act?"

United States Army

My final example contains only a suspicion of dysfunction. It is prompted by a speech presented by General Peter A. Kind of the United States Army to the Software Technology Conference of April 12, 1994, in Salt Lake City, Utah [5]. In this address, General Kind extolls the Army's record in instituting a program of software reuse. The program was difficult to implement but, on the whole, General Kind argues, a great success:

> *Does reuse reduce cost? In the Advanced Field Artillery Tactical Data System it avoided $40 million. The Tactical Communications Interface avoided $5 million, and the Army Command and Control System avoided $480 million. That's a total of $525 million in those three programs.*

Wow. Sounds impressive, and perhaps it is. But I wonder where those numbers came from. They didn't come directly from General Kind who, for all his qualities as a good general, probably makes no pretense of being a whiz with software metrics. They were given to him, I suspect, by workers several levels below. You have to ask the question, Were those workers made more secure in their jobs or in their budgets or in their control of power by the findings they reported? Almost certainly they were. Now imagine yourself in exactly that position. You have been asked to produce a metric showing the savings of reuse, and, by the way, no harm done if the results show *really huge* savings. How would you go about it? Here's a possibility: You measure the cost of producing any particular piece of code, count the number of total times it is used, and compute:

Net Saving = Cost to Produce × (Number of Uses − 1)

So, if there is a module that cost $1 million to produce and it is used fifty times, the net saving is $49 million.

What could possibly be wrong with this? Well, two things. First, it has the dangerous characteristic that the saving is directly proportional to the original production cost. So, if you spend $2 million to produce the very same module instead of $1 million, your saving would jump from $49 million to $98 million. Spend a little more, and you save a lot more.

The second problem is that the calculation doesn't include any indication of benefit. So, a monstrously overpriced module that has little or no benefit might be added to a system that itself has no benefit just to produce a "saving" of enormous proportion.

This is saving in the grand tradition of Blondie who tells Dagwood, "Dagwood, I saved us $300 today by buying three hats at half price." It leaves the American taxpayer musing, along with Dagwood, "Why do I feel so poor in spite of all this saving?"

Of course, I can't prove that the Army used precisely this calculus to arrive at its reported saving, but I suspect they did. If so, it is another example of measurement dysfunction:

meas•ure•ment dys•func•tion *n* : compliance with the letter of a motivational scheme in such a way as to achieve exactly the opposite of that scheme's underlying goals and intentions

"BUT THEY DIDN'T ACT PROFESSIONALLY!"

In each of these cases of measurement dysfunction or suspected dysfunction (even including the Soviet nail factory), you could argue that the workers didn't act professionally, that they really shouldn't have allowed the measurement scheme to influence them to the detriment of the organization's real goals and intentions. But they did. And they always will.

You can't have it both ways on professionalism. You can't expect workers to be totally professional and also expect them to allow themselves to be explicitly motivated by simplistic metric indicators of good performance. Even that prototypical example of professionalism, the medical doctor, will not act professionally if he or she is also trying to work to the numbers: maximizing patients seen per hour, drugs prescribed, specialists referred, sutures and bandages saved, and a host of other numerical indications of success.

The numerical indications of success are what W. Edwards Deming calls "extrinsic motivators." Things like professionalism, pride of workmanship, identification with true organizational success, and pleasure in work well done are "intrinsic motivators." As Deming points out, extrinsic motivators tend to drive out intrinsic motivators. When you direct people to work to the numbers, they do just that. Lost in the shuffle are their own intrinsic values and your organization's real goals and imperatives. The result is sure to be dysfunction.

MANAGEMENT BY OBJECTIVES

Encouraging people to work to the numbers is what the 1960s called Management By Objectives (or MBO). MBO had a brief history as the fad du jour through the early 1970s, and then largely disappeared from the popular business press, though unfortunately not from all our organizations. The problem was that MBO didn't work very well. Companies that tried it didn't prosper; most people who used the scheme were clearly aware of the growing dysfunction it caused.

I think you can see where I'm heading: directly toward my third Disquieting Thought About Software Metrics:

DT#3:	Have we in the software industry through the use of our software metrics programs inadvertently rediscovered Management By Objectives?

I suspect we have. We've stumbled upon a bankrupt concept from the past, and tried to make it work without ever understanding why it didn't work before.

Too harsh? Judge for yourself from the following example. If it looks and smells and tastes and feels like Management By Objectives, maybe it is Management By Objectives.

John Young's 10× Program

In 1987, John Young, then CEO of Hewlett-Packard, announced that HP would achieve a tenfold improvement in a selected set of software performance metrics, including productivity, defect density, and other indicators of proficiency. This thousand percent improvement would become the principal focus of the company's software organizations through 1993.

In 1993, Young announced that the program had been a failure, having achieved only three times improvement on average. But, he allowed, he was thankful for the improvement achieved. Little joke there, much appreciated by Wall Street: Hard-as-nails manager goads people into an astounding 300 percent across-the-board improvement, and then modestly suggests that his program has been a "failure." But Young's assessment was a lot closer to the truth than even he understood.

To get an idea of how 10× could work against the real best interests of HP, imagine a similar scam worked on your child in the classroom. The teacher announces that the students' reading speed "will improve" by a thousand percent over the next few months, and leaves the kids to figure out how they'll do it. They are set up to fail, and sure enough they do fail (and are told so at the end of the period). Not only that, but they knew all along they would fail, that the target was stupidly unrealistic and that they were given nothing that could hope to help them achieve such wonders. How do they feel when it's all over? Cheated, used, and abused.

So, too, at HP. The bad feeling (and flight of professional talent) that resulted from the 10× program are its only real results; the reported 300 percent improvement turns out to be a "trick of the light." HP's real improvement over the period was approximately what it would have been without 10×. Management By Objectives strikes again.

MBO only engenders dysfunction. When a U.S. president announces that "the U.S. will be first in math and science education by the year 2000," the sure result is that the U.S. will not be first nor even significantly better. The most that will happen is some simplistic and relatively meaningless "indicator" may be maximized before everyone turns away in embarrassment. The wild-eyed goals that MBO practitioners favor only assure that meaningful progress, the kind that might achieve real 4 percent or 6 percent improvement, is ignored.

BAD METRICS, BAD SCIENCE

The dark side of measurement that I've presented so far shows how even good metrics can be abused to do real harm, but this is not by a long shot the worst of the story. What concerns me even more is a tendency toward bad metrics and bad science, and the effect these have had on us. We have a long history of guiding ourselves with simplistic indicators that don't stand up to even the most cursory empirical proof. I present one example from the field of medicine and two from our own domain of software development. The medical example is worth exploring in some detail, since it provides a capsule of how bad metrics get established in the first place and how they then prove almost impossible to get rid of. As you will then see, many of the same effects are at work in software metrics.

The National Cholesterol Mania

My least favorite metric of the twentieth century is dietary cholesterol as a predictor of early heart attack. The relationship, if there is one, appears to be extraordinarily weak, and has never been adequately substantiated. Yet millions of Americans have transformed their eating habits to reduce cholesterol intake. Because a belief in low-cholesterol diets is now so deeply ingrained in us all, we need to go back over the subject to see how this has happened. Here is a brief chronology of our national cholesterol mania:

1953:   A study of 5,127 adults in Framingham, Mass., notes that people who die of premature heart attack often have high levels of serum cholesterol in their blood (not quite the same as saying that people with high serum cholesterol in their blood often have premature heart attack). This study also finds that a variation in the intake of high-cholesterol foods has little affect on serum cholesterol. This latter finding was omitted from published reports on the study.

1972:   MR. FIT study (with 12,866 male subjects studied over 10 years, 250 full-time researchers, and a $115 million budget) sets out to prove that lowering intake of high-cholesterol foods can reduce risk of heart attack. The study fails utterly: More people die of heart attack in the low-cholesterol group than in the control group.

1982:   National Cholesterol Education Program is launched anyway. The thrust of the program is severe restriction of high-cholesterol foods.

1987:   National Cancer Institute study (of 12,488 men and women) links lowered cholesterol with increased risk of cancer. Other studies show greater deaths in cholesterol-lowered patients due to stroke and stress-related trauma. Numerous studies show that whatever effect dietary cholesterol has, it is far less important to the heart's health than regular use of moderate amounts of alcohol.

What we know today is that lowering your intake of high-cholesterol foods has a very small effect on your serum cholesterol, and that lowering your serum cholesterol has a problematic effect on your life expectancy. The more you lower your cholesterol, the more likely you are to die of something other than heart attack, but your life expectancy doesn't change much.

Many studies (maddeningly) show that the most rigorous cholesterol reduction methods lead to shorter life expectancy.

In spite of this less-than-compelling evidence, many Americans have drastically changed their eating habits and attitudes. Ordering eggs at breakfast nowadays is likely to get you banished to the Cholesterol Section of the dining room, lest your table mates be subject to too much side-stream cholesterol. We are far more conscious of dietary cholesterol than other factors that have a much stronger impact on life expectancy, like stress, exercise, and moderate alcohol consumption. How did this happen?

There is something far more important than evidence at work here: Our Puritan conviction that foods like ice cream and chocolate and steak and eggs and cheese and whipped cream must be bad for us because they taste good. The more desirable foods are, the more suspect they become. The association of delicious richness with sin and death screams at us from the dessert section of almost any menu: Death by Chocolate, Divine Decadence, Sinfully Delicious Cheesecake. The whole cholesterol hullabaloo confirms our grimmest fears; if these things aren't really bad for us, they should be.

When our doctors lecture us about getting more exercise and lowering stress, we let our eyes glaze over and grunt things like "Sure, Doc, right." But when they speak of the evils of a high-cholesterol diet, we gulp hard and say, "Oh, oh. Tell me more." Doctors are human, too. We are essentially training them to talk less about exercise and stress reduction and more about diet.

There is an important lesson to be learned from all this: *Our disposition to believe what we fear is more important than the quality of the evidence.* It's much easier to "prove" something that people have grimly suspected all along. This factor is almost always present when bad science and bad metrics join together to lead to bad conclusions.

What has all that got to do with software metrics? What would be the equivalent of cholesterol in the software world? Well, how about . . .

Halstead's Software Science Metrics

The software industry has now been through more than a decade of flirtation with the metrics first introduced in Maurice Halstead's *Elements of Software Science* [6]. To date, more than a thousand papers have been published treating different aspects of the Halstead canon. There was even an annual SCORE conference dedicated entirely to Halsteadism. A prominent feature of these papers and conferences was elaboration and refinement of the various lemmas and theorems first set out by Halstead. A non-feature has been empirical confirmation. Most of the articles, like Halstead's book, were entirely analytical. However, there is no empirical body of evidence to show that any of Halstead's software science metrics have anything to do with anything. Halstead occasionally alluded to some empirical work, but researchers who went back over his data have been unable to confirm any of the relationships that Halstead himself seemed to be able to see there. Even his own data wouldn't confirm his findings.

What could be going on here? Why have these metrics achieved so much prominence in spite of the lack of empirical validation? The mumbo jumbo content of software science has played a role here; *Elements* is full of obscure mathematics, Greek letters, untranslated Russian quotes, and logarithms to the base 2. More important, though, is that Halstead set out to prove what many managers had grimly suspected all along: that software was being conducted as an art even though there was a detailed science that should have been used instead. Such managers found themselves asking angrily, "If Halstead is practicing *science,* as he so frequently asserts, then what the hell is it that my programmers are doing?" Not science.

While I'm at it, the Halstead metrics are not the only ones that are long on grimmest fear value and short on empirical confirmation. There is also . . .

Cyclomatic Complexity

Based on the number of people who purport to have used it, Tom McCabe's Cyclomatic Complexity—also called V(G) for some reason now forgotten—is the most successful software metric of all time [7]. Moreover, the paper that introduced it is among the most successful software articles ever written, based on the frequency of citation in the literature. But the metric, though intuitively pleasing, is largely unconfirmed (McCabe's original paper is almost entirely analytical).

The appeal of V(G) is that it gives you a way to spot and rout out complexity. But when you let it guide you to produce alternate designs with lower values, you almost always end up dividing the modules into smaller ones. Now that is a pretty sensible thing to do in general, but it is not really a complexity reduction technique. It's a length reduction technique. You could do the same thing with a much simpler metric, like lines of code: If a module has too many lines, divide it up. V(G) is, most of all, a length metric. Longer modules have higher V(G). If you factor out the hidden effect of length, V(G) is relatively meaningless.

What is the grimmest fear here that predisposes us to believe in V(G)? Again, put yourself in the manager's shoes, and this time imagine yourself to be a manager who is little-versed in software technology. Every time your folks come to you to explain their work, it all seems so complex. Why can't they make it simpler? you wail. Why can't they "keep it simple, stupid"? Your grim suspicion is that all that complexity is artificial. If the artificial complexity could be routed out, the result would be simple enough so that even you could understand it. V(G) to the rescue.

We tend to accept without empirical confirmation metrics that have good intuitive appeal. Shame on us for that. But no shame to the people who first suggest such metrics. I know Tom McCabe, for example, to be thoughtful, competent, and impeccably honest. His original Cyclomatic Complexity paper was a fine piece of work that laid out important directions to be investigated. It doesn't reflect badly on him at all that our industry swallowed the metric whole without first doing the homework suggested by the paper. His integrity is unquestionable.

But such unquestionable integrity is not the general rule in the field of software measurement. That brings us to the topic of . . .

LYING

In our personal lives, lying involves a simple and sincere sounding statement of the exact opposite of the truth: "Honest, Mom, there're never any drugs or alcohol used at these parties." There may be some of this kind of lying at work in software metrics as well, but I suspect it is rare.

What we have to worry about more is a kind of lying that is more often seen in politics. This lying involves sorting through a large amount of data and then presenting those findings that support a preconceived conclusion while systematically suppressing all the rest. This common form of lying does not even have a name, though it needs one. I propose that we call it Limbaughing the data.

> **Lim.baugh** *vt* : to choose selectively from a body of data those items that confirm a desired result and never mention any that might be construed to confirm the opposite

I myself have been guilty of this and will burden you with the story in order to unburden myself of the guilt:

DDT-360

It all began in 1966 when my colleague Gene Levy and I built a small time-shared debugging system on contract for IBM's San Jose office. This product, called DDT-360, was part of a larger effort to produce IBM's CALL-360 product. At the end of the CALL-360 project, IBM announced it had no ongoing interest in the debugging system, which IBM then released to us for $1. I set out to sell DDT-360 to a world that needed it desperately, but didn't yet know it. Of course, what was required to make this sale was some knock-your-socks-off data proving that people who used on-line debugging ended up with far higher-quality products. So I set out to collect that data.

Note that the finding preceded the data. When you let data tell you what it will, you are doing science. When you collect data specifically to prove what you've already decided you want to prove, that is not science, but marketing. No matter. Click-counter in hand, I went looking for my proof.

As has inevitably been my experience, the data proved the opposite of what I wanted. The data showed that on-line debugging led to lower-quality products. This was about as welcome to me as the data showing premature deaths of people on low-cholesterol diets was to the heart researchers. I courageously filed the results under "Lost Data."

What I could prove was that the cost of removing a given bug was lower with on-line debugging than without. This is not at all the same, but it would have to do. I Limbaughed up a case for DDT-360 that emphasized the cost per defect removed and never mentioned that on-line methods produced lower-quality code.

Crime, fortunately, did not pay in this case. Nobody bought the system. So my feelings of guilt, at least, are unencumbered by ill-gotten gains.

Limbaughing the data is not the only kind of lying that is prevalent in our field. There is also another effect, which I call "promotion of credentials."

Problems of the Schools

Maybe you've already come across that dismaying analysis comparing problems of the schools in the 1940s with problems of the schools in the 1980s. In the 1940s, it asserts, the main problems were 1) talking, 2) chewing gum, 3) making noise, 4) running in the halls, 5) getting out of turn in line, 6) wearing improper clothing, and 7) not putting paper in wastebaskets.

By the 1980s, the top problems had become 1) drug abuse, 2) alcohol abuse, 3) pregnancy, 4) suicide, 5) rape, 6) robbery, and 7) assault.

Now there is a surefire indication of the decline and fall of civilization as we know it. The only trouble is that it's a fraud.

Barry O'Neill of Yale University set out to find where that list came from. In the process, he came across hundreds of published versions. Each time he found a new one, he wrote to inquire where the author had gotten the material. Little by little, he homed in on the source. The original source for the two lists was a born-again fundamentalist and campaigner against the public schools named T. Cullen Davis of Fort Worth, Texas. O'Neill asked Davis how he'd come up with the lists.

"They weren't done from a scientific survey," Davis replied. "How did I know what the offenses in the schools were in 1940? I was there. How do I know what they are now? I read the newspapers."

What happened after he began distributing the lists is what's most troubling. They were picked up by fundamentalist author Tim LaHaye and subsequently by activist Phyllis Schlafly, Harvard's Derek Bok, former drug czar William Bennett, former surgeon general Jocelyn Elders, Senator John Glenn, columnists Ann Landers, George Will, Rush Limbaugh, Anna Quindlen, Herb Caen, and Carl Rowan, *The Wall Street Journal,* and CBS News. Each time the list was transferred, its source was likely to be promoted. People who learned it from Phyllis Schlafly quoted it as hers, rather than cite the source that she had cited. Those who got it from George Will quoted it as his. Whenever the propagator had better credentials than the source that he or she cited, new users chose the more credible attribution. Little by little, the Problems of the Schools lists acquired real respectability. This kind of promotion of credentials is out-and-out lying.

Persistent dishonesty is only part of what made the lists live on. They benefited as well from an element of proving what their audience already grimly suspected. To someone who knows in his heart that the schools are going to hell in a handbasket, not much further proof is required.

Software, you might think, is a bit less emotional than the schools. Could there be a promotion of credentials problem in our discipline as well? Consider this:

Nine DoD Development Projects: Where the Money Went

A 1979 report by the General Accounting Office to the U.S. Congress looked at 113 software development contracts let by the Department of Defense (DoD), and attempted to draw some conclusions from them [8]. Buried on page 11 of the report was the graph shown as Fig. 2 on the next page.

Shortly after the report was published, author and colleague Barry Boehm sent me a copy of the graph with the handwritten annotation: "Amusing but deceptive." I tucked it away and didn't think further about it.

I have since encountered that graph perhaps thirty times in presentations and articles. Sure enough, its cited source has varied with the years, each time achieving a bit more prominence. Most recently, it has appeared under the banner of the prestigious Software Engineering Institute. (I have purposely left out the names of those guilty parties who took part in promoting the graph's credentials; the world of software metrics is small and many of these rascals are close personal friends.)

When I recently asked Barry Boehm about the graph, he pointed out that promotion of credentials is only one of the ways in which the graph deceives each new audience. It seems to imply that three-quarters of all DoD contracts result in software that is paid for but never used. However, on page 10 of the report, we see that less than 4 percent of DoD software projects studied were found to be in this category. When presenting this as a gruesome indication of the "really deplorable state of software contracting," the presenter invariably forgets to mention the context. The context was that 113 contracts were studied, and

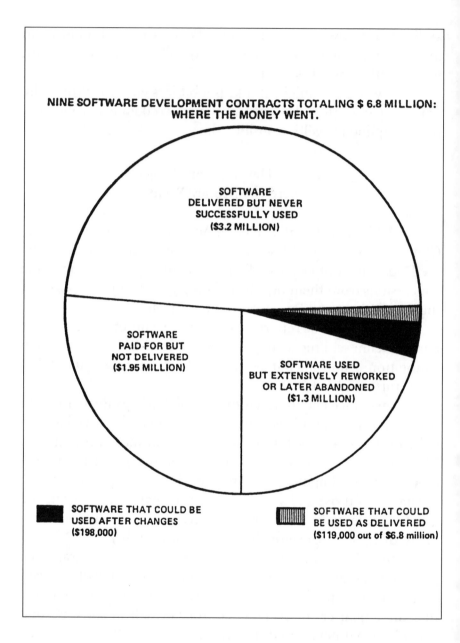

Figure 2. Graph from a 1979 report.

only 9 of them, 9 badly troubled contracts, were included in the pie chart. So the chart shows the characteristics only of contracts known to be in deep bananas, and it specifically doesn't indicate anything about DoD contracts in general. To present the nine-projects graph and not the much more reasonable 4 percent figure is another outrageous example of Limbaughing the data. People who do this should be bitten to death.

Also found here among the usual suspects is Confirmation of Our Grimmest Suspicions. Many of us are more than ready to be shown that government is incompetent to contract software development, and so we don't require a very solid proof.

All of these examples of metrics misuse, dysfunction, bad science, and lying lead me to my fourth Disquieting Thought About Software Metrics:

DT#4:	Is it possible that bad metrics and bad data drive out good metrics and good data?

I have long suspected the truth of this unhappy Gresham's Law of software metrics. Good metrics and good data often have the following unacceptable properties:

- They have too much noise, too much spread around the trendline.
- They have too little impact (proof that object-oriented methods make you 6 percent more productive is too depressing to consider).
- They often prove the opposite of what you want to prove.

Bad metrics and bad data need not be subject to any of these characteristics. They can show tight groupings of data points that prove exactly what you want to prove, say, that object-oriented methods improve your productivity by 600 percent. You can see that the inclination to throw out reasonable and well-collected data in favor of much more useful bad data can be tempting.

THE BASILI STANDARD

Any time you use somebody else's data to prove a cute little point of your own, you run the risk of divorcing the data from the context and thus misrepresenting the true finding. You run the risk of Limbaughing without even knowing it. I suggest that most of those who present the nine-projects graph from page 11 of the GAO report have never even seen page 10 of that same report.

My own record on this subject has been less than perfect. I have often presented data collected by others in order to demonstrate a point that I wanted to make. One day, a member of the audience interrupted to ask a question about a graph of TRW data that I had on the screen. "Can you tell us anything about that third project from the left, Tom? The one that seems to buck the trend. What was going on with that one?" I admitted that I couldn't say a single thing about the third project from the left, nothing at all. And right there in front of that audience, I had the terrible suspicion that if I couldn't answer that kind of question, maybe I shouldn't have been showing those data.

Of course, I'm not the only one who uses other people's data. Everybody does it. Well, almost everybody does it. Among the giants of our profession, I can only think of one who doesn't: Victor Basili. When Basili shows you a graph, you can be sure he can answer any reasonable question about it because he collected the data himself. Basili can do this because Basili collects lots of data. Living up to the Basili standard is harder for the rest of us.

I propose a modified Basili standard for normal people: Only use other people's data when it doesn't confirm your own grimmest suspicions. That will help to keep you out of trouble.

MORE ON CONFIRMATION OF OUR GRIMMEST SUSPICIONS

Data that confirm our grimmest suspicions are almost certainly wrong. The problem is that our willingness to believe disarms our natural defenses against bad data. If we already believe in our hearts that modern television, for instance, is destroying America's youth, then "data" like the following can be very welcome:

This is wrong!

NOT TRUE

Teenage girls who watch Beavis and Butthead are 17% more likely to get pregnant than teenage girls who don't.

Dangerous Non-Fact

(I felt it necessary to surround this dangerous non-fact with disclaimers lest it be picked up by *USA Today*.)

Even your own data should be a source of concern to the extent that the data seem to prove something you believe implicitly, particularly if you are fairly angry about it. Exactly this situation presented itself to me as part of the Coding War Games study that Tim Lister and I conducted from 1984 to 1990. We accumulated a mountain of data showing that people who work in noisy, interrupt-prone space are less effective and more error-prone [9]. When I first spotted the trend, I realized it was something I had always suspected. More than that, I was really irritated about it. Years of frustration over noise and interruptions welled up in me. I was really annoyed and now I had the smoking gun that would allow me to finally do something about the problem. "Yes!" I shouted when I first saw the data. That was a danger sign.

A few weeks later, I happened to meet Victor Basili at a conference. I told him I had some data that were almost scary for the way the data supported something I felt strongly about. I asked his advice: How should I analyze the data in order to be sure I'm not reading more into the numbers than is justified? How can I be sure I'm not snookering myself with statistics? Ever generous, Vic walked me through some of his own procedures for statistical analysis. "Then," he said at the end, "if you *really* have to be sure, do what the rest of us do." "What's that?" I asked. "Fly it past Bill Curtis. If he says it's okay, it is."

That was good advice. It also confirmed my worst suspicion about statistics: It is a discipline so abstruse that no one but Bill Curtis really understands it. (Incidentally, I did call Bill and he said our analysis seemed reasonable.)

THE MISSING METRICS LINK

So far, I have concentrated almost entirely on the dark side of metrics, but there is a bright side as well. The bright side is that most of the problems I've described are treatable with methods that we, the members of the software metrics community, are fully competent to apply. What's required is another kind of measurement.

Before I reveal what I claim is the missing metrics link, let me try the following pop quiz on you: Think of the most recent cost/benefit study performed in your organization. How did it proceed? Chances are, the analysts extrapolated the cost from past cost data, and figured in cost of manpower, cost of quality, cost of materials and travel, cost of risk, cost of possible slippage. When they were done, they published the gross expected cost expressed in dollars, calendar months, person-months, and every other conceivable way. What's missing here? Are those costs the only inputs needed for a cost/benefit study?

The answer, for most organizations, is yes. The cost/benefit study is concerned totally with cost and not at all with benefit. Benefits, if they are mentioned at all, are fuzzy: "The benefit of this system is we gotta have it." or "The benefit is better sales reporting," or "The benefit is competitive advantage."

When benefits are not quantified, it seems almost pointless to me to quantify costs. If the benefit is "We gotta have it," then a perfectly reasonable expression of expected cost is "It will cost what it costs."

By emphasizing the cost characteristics of a project—elapsed time, effort, productivity, and the like—while disregarding the benefit, we send our people the wrong message. We are urging them to get better and better at the kinds of effort that are less and less useful. An organization in the midst of a 10× program like HP's, for example, is totally focused on cost factors, particularly on reducing cost through enhanced productivity. When a really difficult project comes along, one that is bound to result in low productivity, the organization is unlikely to find time for it. But that really difficult project is the one that's probably worth doing.

The paradox at work here is that productivity is often at odds with benefit. Benefit is maximized by taking chances and venturing into new territory. Productivity is improved by familiarity and repetition. When we make software into a production-type activity by "systemizing" the way we build a certain kind of product, we can get much better at building products of that type. (This systemization of software tasks is at the heart of the SEI's Capability Maturity Model.) Is this progress? Why do we need so many products that are so much alike? Have we missed an opportunity to build one meta-product from which many instantiations can be generated instead of building the many clones, each one as a separate project? In most cases, that is exactly what has happened and you can see why. Building hundreds of cloned products can result in low risk and high "productivity" for each of the hundreds of projects. Building one meta-product is highly risky and likely to result in far lower productivity, but the total cost of the one risky project may be much lower.

All the bad press garnered by the Denver International Airport's baggage-handling system is a case in point. You may quibble with the way that the project was administered, but at least the project was worth doing. It took on monumental risks by venturing where no project had gone before. Time will prove that software-controlled robotic systems like the one attempted at Denver International have huge benefit. But of course, since they have an element of experiment, they aren't likely to achieve high productivity along the way.

All our focus on productivity without regard to benefit makes me think this fifth Disquieting Thought About Software Metrics:

DT#5:   Are we learning to do best what we shouldn't be doing at all?

Software is not a production activity. It is a research and development activity, for it is in software research and software development wherein the only real benefits can be produced.

All the attempts to make software into a production activity are doomed to failure. Companies that "succeed" in this are just creating opportunities for the Mike Hammers of the world to suggest, "Instead of pushing your software factory from CMM level three to level four, why not just close it down? It's not building anything very useful anyway." Hammer would call that Business Process Reengineering. I call it Turning the Brain Back to the On Position.

Just as we have learned to make software projects cost-conscious and cost-accountable over the past decade, we now have to relearn how to make them benefit-conscious and benefit-accountable. If the project manager is required to estimate costs and then be responsible for realizing the project within the costs, then someone else (the product manager, perhaps) has to be required to estimate benefits and also be responsible for proving after product delivery that it did indeed achieve its benefits.

The dynamic tension between cost and benefit responsibilities will help our organizations improve. Instead of moving up through artificial Capability Maturity Model levels (which utterly disregard product benefit), we can move toward True Meaningful Productivity:

$$\text{True Meaningful Productivity} = \frac{\text{Total Dollar Benefit Delivered By Product}}{\text{Total Dollar Cost of Building Product}}$$

ONCE MORE WITH FEELING

Presented above are some of the reasons for my own personal journey from ebullient to ambivalent on the subject of software metrics. Along the way, I found some significant truths:

☐ Dysfunction is everywhere; it is the rule rather than the exception.

☐ Metrics can lead to institutionalization, and are often part of an attempt to shoehorn software into a production role.

☐ Metrics are often subverted to be part of a resurgent Management By Objectives.

☐ We, the software metrics professionals, are measuring more and more for Behavior Modification purposes and less and less for Discovery and Steering purposes.

☐ We, the software metrics professionals, tend to measure anything that will sit still for it *except* benefit.

All of this confirms only that the job was harder than we thought it was going to be. But not too hard. A look inside some of our best organizations persuades me that there is reason to hope that software metrics as a discipline still has got great promise. As we move into our second decade of software metrics awareness, I propose that we focus on three back-to-basics principles:

☐ Measure benefit or don't measure anything.

☐ Measure for Discovery. The most promising area for Discovery is the individuals who make up our software teams. In order to measure individuals without erring into MBO and Behavior Modification, we need to organize ourselves to support private self-assessment and self-appraisal. In this scheme, it is the individual who discovers results, not the organization. But the actions that the individual is most likely to take after Discovery are sure to benefit the organization as well as the individual.

☐ Be suspicious of any finding that confirms your darkest suspicions.

REFERENCES

[1] T. DeMarco, *Controlling Software Projects* (Englewood Cliffs, N.J.: Prentice-Hall, 1982).

[2] U. Roze, *The North American Porcupine* (Washington, D.C.: Smithsonian Institution Press, 1989).

[3] Much of the material on dysfunction is inspired by Robert Austin's "Theories of Measurement and Dysfunction in Organizations," Ph.D. Thesis, Carnegie Mellon University, 1994 (forthcoming publication of Dorset House Publishing, New York). See also the two-volume set by my colleagues James and Suzanne Robertson, *Complete Systems Analysis: The Workbook, the Textbook, the Answers* (New York: Dorset House Publishing, 1994).

[4] The essence of this idea was first presented in D. Tajima and T. Matsubara's brilliant 1981 paper, "The Computer Software Industry in Japan," *IEEE Computer,* Vol. 14, No. 5 (May 1981), pp. 89-96. Reprinted in *Software State-of-the-Art: Selected Papers,* eds. T. DeMarco and T. Lister (New York: Dorset House Publishing, 1990), pp. 76-86.

[5] Reprinted as P. Kind, "Software as a Force Multiplier," *CrossTalk, the Journal of Defense Software Engineering,* Vol. 7, No. 7 (July 1994), pp. 2-11.

[6] M.H. Halstead, *Elements of Software Science* (New York: American Elsevier, 1977).

[7] T.J. McCabe, "A Complexity Measure," *IEEE Transactions on Software Engineering,* Vol. SE-2, No. 12 (December 1976), pp. 308-20.

[8] *Contracting for Computer Software Development—Serious Problems Require Management Attention to Avoid Wasting Additional Millions,* U.S. General Accounting Office, FGMSD-80-4, November 9, 1979.

[9] See, for example, T. DeMarco and T. Lister, "Programmer Performance and the Effects of the Workplace," *Proceedings of the 8th International Conference on Software Engineering* (London: 1985), pp. 268-72.

3

Management-Aided Software Engineering

I wrote this with Sheila Brady of Apple Computer for a special issue of *IEEE Software* dedicated to the topic of "Global Vision." I'm not sure we had even one global vision in the process of writing the piece. What we did have was a great number of giggles, some of which, I hope, have come through in the text. We wrote it over the telephone and over the Internet without a single face-to-face meeting.

Sheila Brady is my nomination for World's Best Project Manager. If my life were to depend on the success of a software project, I'd want Sheila to run that project. Apple seems to feel the same way: They regularly put her in charge of their biggest, scariest software projects. If it requires a staff of three hundred or more and it's a bet-the-company-on-this-one project, then it's time for Sheila Brady to step in as manager.

3

MANAGEMENT-AIDED
SOFTWARE ENGINEERING

with Sheila Brady, Apple Computer
Copyright © 1994 IEEE. Reprinted, with permission,
from *IEEE Software*, November 1994.

The bread-and-butter mechanism by which an organization improves is simple enough: People identify best practices that are already working somewhere within the organization and propagate them. This involves no great breakthrough, no new theory. It is basic hygiene. Companies that can do it survive and prosper, and those that can't don't.

Less straightforward is propagation of good practice from one organization to another. The problem here is insularity. We are all so busy holding our cards close to the chest that we have trouble learning from each other.

In the following pages, we present some management best-practice candidates from a small sample of healthy organizations. In addition, we have tried to envision how software management might mature over the next few decades to produce a new generation of best practices.

We have chosen to structure the article as a dialogue, thus preserving our individual voices (also neatly avoiding the necessity of each of us having to sign on to the other's more preposterous ideas of what a best practice is).

1. THE PROJECT POSTMORTEM:
   LEARNING FROM OUR MISTAKES

You might think that a postmortem to examine project successes and failures would be standard practice. It should be, but it

47

isn't. Even the best-run and the worst-run projects (the two kinds that have the most to learn from a postmortem) often leave out this valuable final step.

SB: One of the standard excuses for not running a postmortem is that no one is ever going to pay attention to its findings or, more importantly, do anything differently as a result of reading it. But our experience on Apple's System 7 project was quite the opposite. We put together quite a thorough postmortem report and distributed about 150 copies to the team. Since then, we've distributed an additional 350 copies on an as-requested basis. People ate it up. They loved it. "Oh, wow, look at the dumb mistakes these guys made!" On that effort, we tried our best to probe the underlying problems the project had had to grope with, not just the symptoms.

TDM: As one of your 500 readers, I know that you didn't pull any punches in producing the document.

SB: We didn't, and that was part of its appeal. It set out to be entirely honest and it was. People carried the postmortem into their manager's office and said, "Look. Here's what they did wrong and we're doing the same thing!" Having the problem described in black and white gave them the courage to speak out about the same problem in their project, even to managers who weren't particularly receptive to criticism.

TDM: There are lots of reasons offered for not going back after the project to analyze your successes and failures: no interest, no time, pressures of work, etc. But I sense that the real reason is usually that people are frightened. It's a tribute to management when a postmortem does happen because it means that people under that management felt reasonably safe. When it doesn't happen, it means they didn't feel safe, not safe enough to examine their failures in the light of day.

SB: Of course, that applies much more broadly. It's hard to effect *any* kind of change in an organization where people don't feel safe. You'll never get postmortems to work for you, but you'll never be able to try anything else new and different either.

A postmortem need not be all that threatening. The System 7 postmortem, for example, was a team effort, like the project itself. The team did the postmortem, analyzing its own performance. As manager, my role was to be the scribe, not the judge. I found it was useful to have the postmortem working meetings run by different people at different sessions, and with different subsets of the teams present. The variations in approach and findings were often startling, and always instructive. If you really want to find out about the quality of leadership on the project (your own, for example), have a few sessions where the leaders aren't present. I learned most from some of the meetings that I didn't attend; that was such a comeuppance for me.

TDM: It's important that everybody know the rules. There are a couple of rules to respect:
✓ get everyone involved
✓ give everyone a voice
✓ let people vent their frustrations and make sure they know they will be heard
✓ finally, do something with what you learn; commit to pick the most important lessons and incorporate them into the culture

SB: Now we have a defined process for postmortems at Apple, at least a proposal for one. Bonnie Collier and Peter Fearey have set down in black and white just what steps to take [1]. That, too, helps to make it less threatening. We're now approaching postmortem time for the PowerPC™ project. We'll use the defined process to do the PowerPC postmortem.

TDM: I see that happening more and more. AT&T, for example, has put together a defined process for "retrospectives," as they are called in that culture [2].

SB: The big challenge in the future is to change the mentality to make it okay to raise issues, to point out what isn't working, and to measure what has improved.

TDM: Looking even further into the future, I'd like to know why should we wait until the end of a project to do a postmortem? Why should we wait until people are exhausted and angry to ask them what should we have done differently? I think that the enlightened manager of the future will build mechanisms to do frequent checks on what is working and what is not working.

2. BETTER QUANTITATIVE MANAGEMENT

If we did any other project activity as badly as we set schedules and budgets, the software industry would still be trying to get its first program up and running. What can we do about this lack of discipline?

TDM: Practitioners of any other engineering discipline know that estimating can't be separated from measurement. It is actual measurements of past efforts that enable you to estimate the next. Only in software do people cling to the illusion that it's okay to come up with estimates of the future, even though you've never measured anything in the past.

SB: Measurement is the key. But what do we measure and how do we measure it? Classically, I suppose, we measure whether we are on time and under budget at the end of the project. But how often is this just a gauge of how good the project leader is at sandbagging schedules and padding budget requests? Are those actually appropriate measurements of success? So often, the product is delivered to Marketing to introduce, the engineers are all sent off with their bonuses, and it isn't until later that the sales force discovers we missed the market window, that necessary customer needs are left for Rev 2, and that we won't earn back much more than the original investment on the bally thing. If you ship a worthless, unsellable piece of software on time and under budget, is that a success?

TDM: Just as you suggest that certain kinds of "success" may not be success at all, so too with "failure." The bread-and-butter failure in our industry is a project that is initiated with a hopeless charter (usually a hopeless schedule or budget) and then goes down the tubes one way or another: late delivery, substandard delivery, or total breakdown. Now, clearly, something has failed on such a project. But what?

The pig-in-the-poke explanation we so often buy on software projects is that late delivery is a *performance* failure: Gee, we missed our schedule so we have to become more productive. Wrong. We missed our schedule so we have to learn to set schedules more reasonably. Late delivery is virtually never due to lack of software-building skill or effort. It is a date-setting failure. Learning the wrong lesson from a failure just compounds the failure. If we're going to get any better at estimating, we need to learn that failure to deliver within our estimate is an estimating failure, not a production failure.

SB: Sensible estimates are derived from past observation and measurements. They are then tracked against present measurement. The time to start measuring is at the beginning of the project, not at the end. The most important thing to measure is the burn rate of our most valuable resource: time. Projects that don't do this suffer from a cavalier loss of time in the early stages. The sense of urgency that is so apparent at the end is often hazy and indistinct at the beginning. The cost of time lost is uncertain and unknown. Project members and management are willing to let issues languish for days, even weeks. Yet a week saved in the early days of the project is just as important as a week saved during the rushed and vibrant scurrying moments of final build. (This thought is richly developed in the book *Developing Products in Half the Time* [3].)

How do we, as managers, value that time? How do we urge issues to be closed, and actions to be taken? Of course, there is the old-fashioned way: We nudge the hell out of everyone. To get us off their backs, people grudgingly take action. But how much easier it is to get people to move if they can actually see the value of action rather than avoidance.

TDM: Holding the burn rate up for all to see does this. "Look, we used up one percent of our time today; did we get one percent closer to ship?"

The next most important thing to measure is product inflation. Even a project correctly scheduled from empirical observation can go awry if the underlying proposed product grows during the effort. We need to admit up front that this may happen, and that product size is our principal unknown. Now we make up half-a-dozen project plans to deal with the different realities we may encounter. That moves us to a more healthy focus on indicators that will alert us to growth in product size—

what the indicators are and when they may show up. We can decide up front what we're going to do if the effort turns out to be larger than we expected.

SB: Note that growth in the perceived size of the product is not a performance failure either. It usually means we just didn't know up front how big it would have to be. When we ditch the fallacy of performance failure, we can talk intelligently about what to do.

All too often, the people who are lauded as heroes at the end of the project are those who worked many hours of overtime in a vain attempt to meet outrageously inaccurate schedules. Those who made their estimates carefully and then met them as expected are often ignored as being average contributors. The challenge of the future is to learn to reward good estimating, not just heroic delivery.

3. A WORD ABOUT LYING

We all learned in kindergarten that lying to people isn't nice, so don't do it. You might think that would have put the problem to rest, or at least ensured that it wouldn't be a relevant factor in software project management. Dream on.

TDM: Instead of believing that lying isn't nice so don't do it, we seem to be moving toward a common rule: Don't tell anyone else a lie that you're not willing to tell yourself.

SB: People lie because they have trouble facing up to their own failure. Lying is a kind of flight reaction when you're not so much lying to yourself, as denying. That's worse. Denial is harder to deal with. When you lie to yourself, you really know the truth on some level. In denial, you really *don't* know; you haven't opened the closet door and stared truth right in the face. We human beings have excellent skills that enable us to stay in denial mode for an awfully long time. Objective data are essential to combat denial. If you have only two weeks to delivery and 850 open defects . . .

TDM: The payback for some, admittedly expensive, measurement is that you can deal with denial before it happens. Early on in the project, you ask, What shall we do if there are 400 open defects in March? 500? What will our response be if the defect open rate is such-and-such when we're three months out from delivery? Those are hard questions, but dealing with them up front is easier.

The higher the denial (on the organizational chart), the more it hurts. The first thing you need to do is face up to your own tendency toward denial. Make sure it's not you who is stopping the bad news from moving up the hierarchy. You have to be approachable for the bad news as well as the good.

SB: Dishonesty simply can't be tolerated or rewarded in the work or in the manager herself. As I am a terrible optimist, I've found it very helpful to have a more pessimistic first lieutenant to keep me honest. Perhaps we need to have a bulletin board of "Unspoken Truths" that anyone can post things on, which anyone can read. Just as we assign a "Rat Hole" caller in meetings to call "Time" when a discussion is going off target, perhaps we should identify a "Truthteller" to keep an ear out for signs of people kidding themselves, denial of critical issues, or an unwillingness to listen when someone is trying to say the unsayable.

TDM: This is the role of Devil's Advocate, a role that was tragically missing on the Challenger mission, for example, and on most other disastrous projects.

SB: It's not enough to deal with the problem in the manager's own little heart. Denial at the team-leader level is what frightens me most: One of my teams is in trouble, and people underneath know it, but the channel isn't open enough for them to come and tell me. So my job is to smell it out and build a level of trust.

People aren't good at having painful conversations. It's all too easy to fall into some level of denial. The manager has to make it okay to talk about bad things. No anger is allowed. That just stops the flow. We don't have any extra calories to burn being furious.

4. GETTING THE MOST OUT OF A DAY

The more stress we're under to deliver quickly, the more important it is that we manage time, our most important resource, sensibly. Oddly, though, sensible time management seems to be the first "luxury" to be trimmed when the pressure builds [4].

TDM: Ask almost any project manager how to get more out of a day and he or she is likely to talk about overtime. I am gradually coming to the conclusion that there is no such thing as overtime. Oh, right, it might make sense to call people in on one Saturday to construct a build or to work on a specific bug, but extended periods of overtime are likely to be counterproductive.

SB: Projects without overtime? Convince me. Please.

TDM: Overtime, since it puts the project under anaerobic stress, is like sprinting; it might make sense in a short race, but none at all in a marathon. Our typical projects are much too long to benefit from much sprinting. The long-term price we pay for overtime is burnout, and the possible loss of our best people. The gain, of course, is short-term, which explains why we're tempted to make such a costly trade-off. Overtime has an additional cost that is felt almost immediately: Because it focuses us obsessively on the product and not the process, it turns our attention away from even the most obvious process flaws, the most obvious causes of wasted time. Show me a project working extended periods of overtime, and I will show you a project that is wasting far too much of the normal workday.

SB: People will often tell you that they work overtime because the after-hours are so much more work-conducive. They're free from the midday craziness.

TDM: By encouraging overtime, managers dodge their responsibility to make the craziness go away, so that people can get real work done during normal hours. As a young manager, I took great satisfaction from seeing my people work late into the night. I was comforted that they were giving their all for the project, so the project would certainly succeed. Today, I'm more doubtful. I suspect the typical software engineer doesn't work overtime to make the schedule, but in order not to feel so bad about not making it.

SB: Part of the midday craziness that overtime workers are avoiding is meetings. We have too many of them and too many people at each one. When someone isn't present, the others will often complain, "Why isn't so-and-so here?" On the surface, it looks like a legitimate complaint; we all may be wasting our time if one of the key decision makers isn't present. But the same complaint is often heard when the missing person isn't key. I've begun to feel that what the complainer is really saying is that the missing colleague should be here *as punishment*. Hey, if the rest of us have to sit through this meeting, why should so-and-so be let off?

TDM: We think of meetings as information interchange sessions, but they also serve as a kind of corporate ritual [5]. A staff meeting in which people take turns talking to the boss, with nobody else interested in or listening to each other, is a pure ritual. The more ritual you need as a manager, the more of your people's time is used up doing nothing but keeping you secure.

SB: It's an accomplishment to let even one valuable person skip a meeting. We all need to realize this. The fewer people, the better. Best of all is skipping some meetings entirely, the ones that serve only a ritual purpose. The key to keeping meetings small is the agenda. If you don't have one at all, everyone will *have* to show up [6].

TDM: If you generally don't stick to your agendas, everyone will have to come just in case you wander into their subject area.

SB: The biggest cost in software development will always be salary. You pay nothing for tooling, your manufacturing overhead is practically nothing, and your biggest capital expense is often $4,000 for the latest PC and a couple hundred bucks to stock the fridge with Mountain Dew®. The real cost is paying for the software engineer's time. So any moment of that time we can save has immediate payback.

What is it about a software engineer that is so unique, so special, so valuable? At the heart of all the designing, writing, testing, documenting, and debugging that an engineer does is the creative act. The cost of doing anything that cannot be described as the act of creation is, baldly, time and money wasted. To me, this points to the value of software development tools. Anytime a software engineer is doing grunt work, there is an opportunity for a clever person to figure out how to let a tool do the work instead of an expensive engineer. This applies to all the phases of software development, from designing, writing, testing, documenting, and debugging, to archiving.

One of the best time-savers I've seen, especially on large projects, is to add a roving tools specialist—a person who's given the latitude to develop tools that save engineers' time. There is always room to improve any development environment by the addition of a tool to do more of the grunt work and to leave the engineer with more time to create. Imaginative and effective tool writers, just like great quality engineers, are worth their weight in gold. A great debugging tool or even something as simple as a formatting tool can produce enormous savings in time. Also, the project engineers work better, knowing that their time is so highly valued.

5. INVESTMENT/DISINVESTMENT

Pop quiz: Given that an increasingly global economy is trying to take your customers away, which do you do:

☐ Invest? or

☐ Disinvest?

TDM: There is no way to make sense on the topic of good management practice without coming to grips with the issue of investment and its opposite, disinvestment. If you dance around that topic, you end up making pronouncements that may be true but irrelevant; people may follow all your advice and fail anyway (and never understand why).

American companies in the 1990s are going through an orgy of disinvestment. This is particularly true of big companies (which partly explains why all the growth in our economy is coming from the small-cap sector).

What gets disinvested is not so much trucks and machines as people. Companies that are disinvesting today are plundering their past investment in human capital in order to show an apparent profit in the next quarter. The human capital is understandably threatened by this. People don't feel safe when disinvestment is in the air.

The reason this issue matters is that what distinguishes good management is its ability to effect change, and the people who work under that management won't let change happen if they don't feel safe. If they feel threatened, they will fight tooth and nail to hold change at bay. Who would want to experiment with tiger teams or cleanroom development or frame-based engineering or anything new for that matter, while there are madmen prowling through the corridors looking for someone to blame or someone to ax?

SB: Everywhere I go, I hear words of disinvestment: "We have to get more for less!" or "Let's hire contractors, so that we don't have to pay employee benefits!" Six months later, what do you know? Those contractors are walking out the door, with six months of your training and experience under their belts and getting better jobs at a competitor. Meanwhile, you're stuck hiring and training some new contractor. Does this make sense? Or I'm told, "Let's split ourselves up into business units. Everyone has to make a profit next quarter!" Six months later, you discover all your projects are short term, and nothing you do couldn't be duplicated in a garage shop by a couple of college computer nerd dropouts.

Another that I hear is, "Let's get rid of all this bureaucratic overhead!" Then software engineers no longer have people to build their software tools, or write their expense reports, or make their travel arrangements, or help track their bugs, or wrestle with the project scheduling program, or edit their documentation, or fix their hardware, or order their hardware, or order a whiteboard, or send out for dinner on the late nights. Instead, the software engineers spend their time doing all the above, and spend far less time walking boldly across their sea of code.

The answer is not to pare and scrape until every project can barely stand for the lack of flesh on it. To quote an old wise friend, "We must limit our opportunities!"

TDM: Particularly in the area of disinvestment, we need to limit our opportunities.

SB: That doesn't mean we should throw money away on frivolities. To hell with the mahogany-trimmed cafeteria! Who needs Tina Turner at the holiday party! (A decent-sized investment in Nerf® pistols, however, is only sensible.)

TDM: So, what to do about disinvestment? At least, we can name it. Talk about it. Know it for what it is.

SB: Better to turn our attention to the tough question of what is worth investing in while we're in this difficult climate? Then pick a few projects and fund them for success: Do four truly astounding projects really well, instead of thirty that creep and stumble along, as everyone mumbles, "Oh, yes, I have a great feature under my overcoat here somewhere."

We have to take fewer, bigger risks, and set those efforts up for complete success.

6. MANAGEMENT ACCOUNTABILITY

When lowest-level developers realize that any schedule slippage or poor product quality will be judged *their* fault, they are left to wonder: What could ever go wrong that would be the boss's fault?

SB: What does it mean to *be* accountable if you are never *held* accountable? All the classic crimes of management —sloppiness, lack of efficiency, wasting of resources, and lack of compassion or understanding of the work-force—stem not from managers who are unwilling to be accountable, but from managers who aren't willing to hold someone (themselves, in this case) accountable. "To be" is such a passive verb, just waiting around, hanging out on the street corner humming, "Accountable, that's me!" "To hold" is a much more active verb. So, many managers see themselves as accountable, but does any manager really measure the final result and hold the final product up for scrutiny?

TDM: Niklaus Wirth had a lovely slant on this when he man-aged the Lilith project. He would tell his young team leaders when it was time to make a date commitment: "I'm not asking you for an estimate; I'm asking you for a promise." That put everything in a different light. Making a promise to Niklaus Wirth is not something one takes lightly. The act of promising makes you hold yourself accountable.

SB: A lack of accountability flows right from the top. If the top dog isn't willing to hold herself and her folks accountable for their actions, how can she ever expect that they, in turn, will take the effort and time to make sure they understand what their objectives are and what the definition of success is? By her actions, she defines how people will be valued. If she never sets a metric in place for a goal, then her folks know immediately that they can ignore the goal. On the other hand, if a metric is carved in stone, and the stone is set on the boardroom table, and all must pay homage to that stone at the weekly status meeting, then you can bet that goal will stay fresh in everyone's mind.

TDM: All that has to do with winning, but we also need to discuss losing here. Lots of projects fail; project bankruptcy rate can go as high as 25 percent for large projects [7]. Yet organizations are inclined to judge themselves by how well they manage those projects that do succeed. They're missing the point. What distinguishes the best organizations and best managers is not just how well they do on their successful efforts, but how well they contain their failures. You can't do that if you won't even consider the possibility of failure.

The can-do mentality (generally good) makes it hard to come directly to grips with the real possibility of defeat (always bad). Can-do managers are eager to know what's wrong in their projects *as long as those things are correctable,* but they don't allow even a discussion of the problems that can't be fixed. Thus, if there is a line drawn in the sand (for example, on-time delivery, no excuses), all dialogue about the possibility of failure breaks down. People are discouraged from even *considering* failure; to think about it at all is judged to be defeatist. This is where accountability really matters: If you're sitting on top of a project that is failing and everybody under you knows it but you don't know it, that's your own fault. You've made it impossible for bad news to move up the hierarchy.

SB: I don't want can-do management to turn into can't-do management, but not allowing failure to be discussed is just managerial denial again. Denial doesn't help any more at work than it does at home.

7. LEADERSHIP STYLES

We all know leadership must be a good thing because it features so prominently on those inspirational plaques and pictures that managers order from the airline magazines. Isn't there more to leadership than plaques and pictures?

TDM: No.

SB: Oooh, cynical. There is a book of inspirational quotes floating around our shop that is not much better than those awful plaques. But it does serve a function of comic relief. When we realize we've wasted weeks on some dumb thing and everybody is depressed as hell, then someone will pick the book up and read a selected idiocy.

TDM: "Only by spreading your wings can you soar to great heights."

SB: You've read it! Always good for a giggle. Then the work can go on. Humor is a nontrivial element of leadership. One of the leaders I most respected made wonderful use of humor. He wasn't a great leader in other ways—he was positively lazy—but he made humor work for him, particularly in difficult situations. And then I think of someone else who was hard as nails, and had a terrific nose for [expletive deleted]. He could review material that he'd never seen before and in five minutes ask those very questions that would make you shake in your boots. He'd get right to the weakest element of your presentation. He was a great leader in that sense, but flawed in other ways.

TDM: Your role model for leadership, if I get your drift, is a composite of qualities of many managers.

SB: It is. No one of the managers I've had incorporated all of the qualities I value in a leader. I had to learn not to reject the whole manager when there were obvious flaws, but to find and learn from the good characteristics. Then you put it all together in your own way, your own style.

My own leadership style starts with the word *listening*. I can't set myself up as the person who always knows what to do, but when we're stuck, I can usually find someone who has a good idea about what we could do. The most important thing I do is listen. It's important that a manager act as well as listen, but listening comes first.

TDM: Listening is your mechanism for pushing control downward, so decisions get made at the right level.

SB: The project leader's main job is to make sure the right people make the right decision at the right time. The leader can't be the one to make all the decisions.

TDM: A leader is different from a controller. When leadership fails, it's often because the leader keeps the power to make all the decisions. We work in hierarchies—that's what an organization chart is: a hierarchy of authority—but we have to beware as we move up the chart not to think of it as a hierarchy of moral superiority. That attitude gulls us into believing we can, even must, make all the decisions ourselves.

SB: For me, leadership is grounded in very basic human values: honor, integrity, the belief that might does not make right, a refusal to compromise on values. Take integrity as an example: I can only be confident of myself as a leader to the extent I can believe in my own sense of integrity. It is all tied up with a funny kind of guilt: The last thing I want is for some programmer to be able to say to me, "See, you lied to us." I don't ever want that to happen to me. Everyone knows that is important to me.

TDM: By showing your colors about integrity, you open yourself up to the people who look to you for leadership. You give them power. They understand that they can hold you to your values, to the common value set, and that they can depend on that. It sounds dangerous, this giving away of power, and yet without power sharing, there can be no such thing as leadership.

SB: Sharing power and pushing decisions down in an organization require that you assemble the right team. That, too, is an act of leadership, not just to get the strongest talents, but the strongest *mix* of talents: novices with something to prove, people with a marketing bent, interface and quality types, mavericks. Mix it up.

TDM: Again, that *sounds* dangerous. Diversity can be threatening to a manager. After all, if we want everyone to move toward the same goal, maybe we ought to stick with people who are all the same. But that can be fatal.

The problem with diversity is that certain of those diverse types might weigh in against what you the manager want to do. How can that be good? The key is to realize that some resistance to your ideas is positively vital. Jerry Johnson of the Menninger Business Institute puts this most clearly with his "resistance continuum," made up of seven identifiable levels shown in Fig. 1 [8].

Your worst inclination is to think of the first level, the Blindly Loyal, as your only friends and everyone else as enemies. But levels two through six are your real allies. You need the people who are somewhat opposed, skeptical, even fearful, to help your ideas fly. Those at

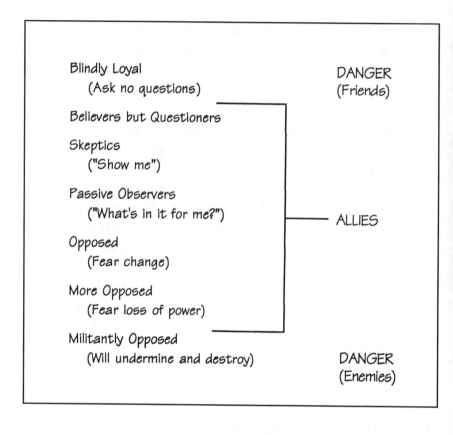

Figure 1. Resistance continuum.

the extremes, blindly for you or blindly against you, are both dangerous. Enlisting the middle levels as allies is a defining act of leadership.

8. CO-LOCATION

Has the advent of CASE, groupware, video conferencing, and extended multimedia e-mail made it possible to develop complex systems with a physically distributed project team?

TDM: I don't think so. Some form of wide-band interaction facility might help if you and your teammates had to work in widely separated locations. You'd require it, just as you'd need a space suit to go moonwalking. But all the technical gimmickry in the world doesn't give you the equivalent of side-by-side interaction.

At least when you go moonwalking, you *know* you're pushing the envelope. I worry about the manager who sets up a project with a few people in Modesto and the rest in Cracow and then thinks that fancy technology will make up for the separation. It doesn't.

SB: As part of the System 7 postmortem, we found many examples of the value of "co-location" (our word for keeping the team together) as an absolute essential. After the 1989 earthquake, we had to evacuate a building with the entire 7.0 team in it to six other smaller sites. Many of the bonds that began to forge between different groups were broken. We took great pains to pull the groups back together again. I believe that we lost months of time in our schedule due to simple miscommunications that weren't caught with day-to-day interactions.

TDM: Interaction at a distance isn't really interaction at all, just as phone sex isn't really sex. If software development were just coding and debugging, we might get away with some kind of groupware, but the bread-and-butter activity of a software engineer is talking to another person. That's how we spend nearly half our time [9]. Communicating across a distance probably doubles the cost and doubles the risk.

SB: There is temporal co-location to consider as well. If the people on the project don't work the same hours, it is the same as if they were working in different places. You see the results in their e-mail:

A (10 A.M. Monday): Did you look at that bug?
B (5 P.M. same day): What bug?
A (10 A.M. Tuesday): The bug I sent you with my last message!

B (5 P.M. same day):   Oh, *that* bug. No, that's in the gizmo manager. Tell the gizmo folks about it.

9. ENDGAME: SHIP HAPPENS

How does the manager's role change as the ship date approaches?

SB: No matter how enlightened you are in your overtime policy, in the endgame it all gets away from you as people begin driving themselves. There is a lot less sleep, tensions are high, and the team acts like a family that has spent too long a holiday together. Your job at this point is to maintain an even balance, to act as the adult.

TDM: Time for Theory Y. Anyway, not Theory X.

SB: Some people's workload should have slowed down as you move toward the ship date. If that isn't so, if everyone still has a million things to get done before delivery, that just says your schedule was all wrong.

TDM: And was from the beginning. If *nobody* has slack at the end, you know there wasn't enough time for even the best performers to finish on schedule. In those cases, you have to face the music and declare some slip.

SB: Assuming the schedule was not all wrong from the beginning, then some folks should be finishing up well in time. People then become fungible to some degree, and you can really be creative about reassignment. You can say, "This guy is clear, can't he help you? I know he's not *the* expert, but he's yours if you can use him." Up against a ship date, people are very willing to help, even willing to be helped.

TDM: People know so much more at the end that they're often very useful even outside their own specialty areas.

SB: Endgame is also a time to look for a key strategy that isn't working for you. You have to ask, without leveling a lot of blame, What is the rational behavior *now?* Is the strategy that I set up nine months ago still the right strategy? Probably not.

TDM: The mistake we make in the endgame is to think that it's too late for strategy and that we have to stop being managers and become cheerleaders.

SB: Instead, it's a time for creative problem solving. You've learned a lot more about your people over the course of the project. You know who has come through for you time and again. So it's reasonable to acknowledge this and do some shuffling around. The decisions you make at the end are often your best calls: You go with your strength.

TDM: It seems obvious, but it's not: The most important thing the manager can do at the end is to keep managing.

REFERENCES

[1]   B. Collier, P. Fearey, L. Johnson, and M. Warner, *AppleSoft Post-mortem Process, Version 1.1,* Apple Computer (Cupertino, Calif.: April 1994).

[2]   P. Sciacca, *Retrospective: A Time for Reflection on Process Effectiveness at the Conclusion of Product Production and Delivery,* AT&T (Columbus, Ohio: February 1994).

[3]   P.G. Smith and D.G. Reinertsen, *Developing Products in Half the Time* (New York: Van Nostrand Reinhold, 1991). See Chapter 3 in particular.

[4]   See Tracy Kidder's book *The Soul of a New Machine* (Boston: Atlantic-Little, Brown Books, 1981) for a fascinating description of what can happen to people involved in a project that's conducted under incredible time pressure.

[5]   R.R. Ritti and G.R. Funkhouser, *The Ropes to Skip and the Ropes to Know* (New York: John Wiley & Sons, 1987).

[6]   D.C. Gause and G.M. Weinberg, *Exploring Requirements: Quality Before Design* (New York: Dorset House Publishing, 1989). See especially Chapter 8.

[7]   C. Jones, *Assessment and Control of Software Risks* (Englewood Cliffs, N.J.: Prentice-Hall, 1994).

[8]   J.W. Johnson and G. Swogger, "Resistance Continuum," Menninger Business Institute, private correspondence, 1992.

[9]   G.M. McCue, "IBM's Santa Teresa Laboratory—Architectural Design for Program Development," *IBM Systems Journal*, Vol. 17, No. 1 (1978), pp. 4-25. Reprinted in *Software State-of-the-Art: Selected Papers*, eds. T. DeMarco and T. Lister (New York: Dorset House Publishing, 1990), pp. 389-406.

Sheila Brady is Program Manager for Software and Development Tools on the PowerPC project at Apple Computer. Before that, she served as project leader for various releases of Macintosh System Software: the 3.2 release, the release supporting the Mac SE, the Mac II, the MultiFinder Release, and System 7.0. She has lived in California all her life, is a graduate of University of California at Berkeley, and vacillates wildly between taking everything too seriously and taking nothing seriously enough.

4

LEAN AND MEAN

The great vogue of the 1990s seems to be becoming "lean and mean." Am I the only one who thinks this is dumb?

4

LEAN AND MEAN

Not previously published.

I get uncontrollable giggles when people tell me their organizations are "lean and mean." They say it in the most ponderous tones. They wrinkle their brows earnestly, and look me right in the eye. "We're lean and mean here," they say. They say this even though they themselves are overweight and positively sweet. And that's only the first of the contradictions.

Why would an organization want to be mean? The word describes an assortment of qualities, none of which seems to my mind to be very desirable. From my *Random House Unabridged Dictionary* (2nd ed.):

> **mean** *adj* **-er, -est.** 1. offensive, selfish or unaccommodating; nasty; malicious. 2. small-minded or ignoble. 3. penurious, stingy or miserly. 4. inferior in grade, quality or character. 5. low in status, rank or dignity. 6. of little importance or consequence. 7. unimposing or shabby. 8. small, humiliated or ashamed

If your organization is already these things, I suggest you start looking for a job. If it's not yet mean, shouldn't you and all the good people who work with you be fighting the trend in that direction for all your worth? If you don't, you're likely to end up working for a company that is small, humiliated, and ashamed.

By citing mean as a desirable corporate quality, I suppose managers are really trying to stress competitiveness. But we can be extraordinarily competitive without taking on any of the attributes mentioned in the dictionary definition. We all learned as school children that that is the essence of sportsmanlike conduct: Pull out all the stops to win, but don't sacrifice a single principle of civilized behavior along the way. That is not just sensible advice for school kids; it's sensible advice for adults as well.

Companies that set out to be mean are not just mean to their competitors. They are not even *principally* mean to their competitors. Mostly, they are mean to their employees. Magically, the goal of becoming lean and mean excuses managers when they fire loyal and competent workers, degrade people for honest failure, or push staff members to work mind-numbing hours at the expense of family. It excuses them for setting up a culture of fear. But these things aren't excusable, and organizations that do them don't get healthier as a result; they just get sicker and sicker and sicker.

Early in my career, I worked at a bank that was envious at the success of its competitor, Citibank. "They're hard as nails over there," our president observed. "They fire people at the drop of a hat and squeeze twenty-four hours a day out of their people. The place is run by a heartless gestapo. We have to learn to be like that." They did.

Learning to be a heartless gestapo manager is the easy part. The hard part is surviving the aftermath. None of them did at this particular bank, and the bank itself has never prospered since.

If meanness is a stupid goal, leanness isn't much better. Becoming lean means cutting salaries, trimming overhead, and making the workplace more spare, more crowded, and less comfortable. In short, it means making people's jobs less enjoyable in every conceivable way. If you find yourself working at a plastic desk in unnatural light, without proper clerical support, surrounded by bothersome noise, something is wrong.

Your office at home, the place where you settle down for a few hours a month to pay your bills, is not so grim. Why would an organization provide for its people so much more stingily than people provide for themselves? There is a very good reason: The organization is failing. Becoming lean is a not a sign of future health, but of present failure.

The ultimate way to achieve leanness is downsizing or, to put it more bluntly, firing lots of people more or less at random. This is what my colleague Ken Orr calls "organizational bulimia." Downsizing is exactly the opposite of what management has been chartered to achieve. The natural goal for almost any business is upsizing. Downsizing programs are clear admissions of upper management failure. (Yet, somehow, it's never upper management that gets downsized.)

Lean and mean means sick and angry. Maybe that's what many organizations have become, but it's time to stop pretending that it was ever a desirable goal.

5

STANDING NAKED IN THE SNOW
(VARIATION ON A THEME BY YAMAURA)

I first met Tsuneo Yamaura in Boston in 1988. He was part of the team of translators assembled by Tomoo Matsubara to wrestle the text of *Peopleware* into Japanese [1]. As you might imagine, such an idiomatic book was particularly difficult to translate. How to render "Furniture Police" or "Hornblower Factor" or "Umbrella Steps" into a foreign language? I don't know if all the subtleties made it into Japanese, but I do know that they all made it into Yamaura's head. He didn't need to have a single gag or allusion explained. Just in case we wondered if he had understood, he had a story to tell and a lesson of his own on the theme of each one of ours. They were all wonderful.

Someday, perhaps, we'll have a book from this young man, and perhaps it will be full of the material he shared with us during the translation project. For the present, though, we have only one short English-language essay from Yamaura, his marvelous "Standing Naked in the Snow," which appeared in the January 1992 issue of *American Programmer* [2]. The following essay is my response to Yamaura's piece.

5

STANDING NAKED IN THE SNOW
(VARIATION ON A THEME BY YAMAURA)

A few years ago in this space, my friend and colleague Tsuneo Yamaura of Hitachi Software, Ltd., wrote a charming piece entitled "Standing Naked in the Snow." Yamaura is a young man of whom I expect great things. He combines freshness of insight and humor with an elegance of expression that transcends language barriers. In his 1992 article, he described the world of a beginning first-level manager in a large Japanese software engineering company. It was his own world he was writing about, and the portrait he drew was credible. What he told us was as fascinating for its likeness to the Western counterpart as for its difference. Yamaura related the trial by fire one goes through to attain the first management position, and he went on to describe how he learned to deal with the young people who reported to him, how to challenge them, and how to buoy them up whenever they stumbled.

For all the useful insights in the piece, what has stayed with me most is the device of the title: the image of the novice manager "standing naked in the snow." It is an image that has haunted me ever since, as much today as when I first read Yamaura's words. I was that novice manager once. I was standing naked in the snow.

No wonder that new managers feel so exposed. They are catapulted into management for proficiency in skills like coding and debugging and program design and optimization, skills that are made instantly inadequate by the act of their promotion. The skills required in their new position are only vaguely understood. In my case, I couldn't even have made a decent list of them. I didn't even know their names. I still had code on my breath.

What do you do (what did you do?) on your first day as a manager? Of course, you do much the same sort of thing you did the day before. You write a little code, do some debugging, tune up the spec. But now you're not doing this so much to get the work done as to show yourself—the Big Cheese, for god's sake—doing real work. You show your people how important the work is by pitching in and doing it. You show them how much they should care by caring yourself to an obvious extreme. You demonstrate the value of quality by producing quality modules and test plans and test sets. You entice people to work long hours by working the longest hours yourself. Thus is born one more Lead-By-Example Manager.

If you're like me, you quickly convince yourself that this must be the essence of management. But it isn't. If I could impress only one thing on you today, it would be this: Lead-by-example management is not management at all.

THE STORY OF O.

Consider the story of Mr. O., an extreme case of lead-by-example management. He manages some hardware types, so he does some of the same things that they do: tinkers with bread-boarded circuits and tries to invent neat solutions to real problems. He manages analysts so he gets on the phone to the users and haggles details of the requirement. He manages programmers, so he slings a little code, too, propping up the C++ manual by the side of the screen as he labors on long into the night. He stays later, tries harder, pushes himself more, and gets more done than anyone who works for him. What an example!

Yes, Mr. O. is an impressive example of a multi-talented, multi-skilled worker. But as a manager, he is something far less admirable: a textbook example of what psychologists call "over-functioning." The problem with over-functioning is that it causes those around you to under-function. The harder you try to present a perfect example, the more the folks who work for you come to feel they'll never live up to your expectations and so there is no use even trying. The harder you work, the more you undermine their own satisfaction at doing a job well. The harder you work, the more they become automatons, putting in the minimum to get themselves through each day.

We haven't seen the worst yet. What happens when Mr. O. is promoted to a higher level of management? Now he has sales people reporting to him as well, so his day is further fragmented as he tries to make a few sales calls in addition to everything else. There is now a new layer of management inserted between Mr. O. and the worker level. This new layer is made up entirely of lead-by-example managers. Of course, it is: If the Kingpin still does the functions normally performed at the bottom, what else is the subordinate manager to do? Soon, we have a whole hierarchy of such managers: sales managers selling, development managers developing, training managers training. What's missing from this picture? I'll tell you what's missing: management.

SO WHAT IS MANAGEMENT, ANYWAY?

Management is a set of *catalytic* activities that enable people to work productively and happily. Like a catalyst in chemistry, the manager's contribution is not itself transformed into product, but it is entirely necessary for the transformation of others' efforts into product.

The easy part of the manager's job has to do with control and coordination. The hard part has to do with such human considerations as motivation, harmony, teamwork, personal growth, and job satisfaction. It is this second category, human affairs, that the lead-by-example manager never gets around to.

The manager's most important task is system design. But it is not the product system that the manager needs to design, it is the system that builds that product: the project. Designing the project means hiring the right people, putting them in the right place, building teams, keeping people's spirits up, and redesigning when the result is improvable. Great managers don't even end up steering their projects. They don't have to. If they've succeeded in their design, they have constructed a project that knows how to find its own way.

WHY WE LEAD BY EXAMPLE

Managers who lead by example will give you an impassioned rationale, as diverse as it is heartfelt:

✓ "People want to see me doing the same things they're doing."
✓ "I love the satisfaction of the work. I can't get enough of it."
✓ "There's nobody else available to do this job. I have to help out."
✓ "I'm no elitist. I'm not afraid to get my hands dirty."
✓ "We're lean and mean here—everybody pitches in."
✓ "A manager who just manages is pure overhead."

This boils down to a denigration of management. It suggests that the work going on under the manager's direction is somehow respectable, but management of that work is not. The work itself confers a kind of nobility, and management doesn't.

You only need to work once under a great manager to learn that there is no more noble work than enabling others to succeed. Management is as creative and satisfying as anything that goes on below. It is also harder. I think that is the real reason we lead by example. It lets us do easy things instead of hard things. It lets us work on tasks where our competence is a hundred percent instead of those human relationship tasks where our competence is barely there at all.

As a young manager, I knew I really wasn't competent to design teams, to work out convoluted human problems, to motivate people who were feeling sulky and depressed. Of course, I wasn't. Nobody is. Nobody is a hundred percent competent in these complex domains. That means someone who is less than one hundred percent competent (and knows it) has to take the work on. That's hard and takes real guts. We have a name for the person who is courageous enough to take on these tasks. We call such a person "Boss."

A PERSONAL NOTE

I have had the privilege of working under nine great managers. None of them ever led by example. They never did anything except the hard stuff. They designed projects with loving care, tinkered with the peopleware, helped communities to form, and refined and admired their creations. When there was success, they celebrated human triumph.

In spite of my amazing luck in having such bosses, I still made the dumb mistake that other new managers were making. I led by example. I never got any good at all until I finally shook the habit. One fine day, I made a list of all the things my subordinates were doing. And I swore to myself that whatever I did from then on, I would not do one single thing on that list. I was coming to grips with the real reason I had led by example in the past. It was because I was afraid. I admitted that when I had done the work that those under me were charged with doing, it was nothing more than a retreat from my real responsibilities.

MANAGERS, TAKE HEART

Leading by example is not a disgrace. It's just a catastrophe. When you find yourself someday, standing naked in the snow, take heart. Think of those who have gone before you and succeeded. Think of the beautiful little communities they built, of the satisfactions they made possible. What lies ahead is not easy, but it's wonderful. Of course, you're not entirely competent to do it, but then neither is anyone else. Don't turn away from this, the ultimate challenge. This is the stuff of which great managers are made.

REFERENCES

[1] T. DeMarco and T. Lister, *Peopleware: Productive Projects and Teams* (New York: Dorset House Publishing, 1987).

[2] T. Yamaura, "Standing Naked in the Snow," *American Programmer*, January 1992.

6

IF WE DID ONLY ONE THING TO IMPROVE ...

In the effort to become more productive, everything matters. Lots of things matter a lot, but what matters most?

6

IF WE DID ONLY ONE THING
TO IMPROVE ...

Not previously published.

This past spring, I began my thirtieth year as a software project consultant.

There is a routine to my consulting engagements that goes something like this: arrival, meeting with client, coffee, small talk, organizational chart, closed door, discussion of problems, tour of premises, work with two or three unit managers, lunch, meetings with the teams, dinner with upper management, subsequent days of working with developers, and finally a debriefing. In the debriefing, I reflect on what I've seen. I say what looks good and what looks not so good. Then I offer the best advice I can in the following form: "If my life depended on the success of this project, here are the things I would do. . . ."

The list is made up of doable tasks, but none is easy, the easy options having usually been exhausted long before. A typical prescription will consist of half-a-dozen action items. I lay them out as clearly and persuasively as I know how, and then settle back for a reaction.

The reaction, when it comes, is often in the form of negotiation. One or another of the items on my list is just too hard to swallow. "Couldn't we somehow succeed without . . . ?" The bitterest of the bitter pills is named and then we put our heads together to work on the alternatives.

An extreme form of this negotiation is the manager who asks, "What if we did only *one* thing to improve our chances of success? What would it be?" In my relative youth, this question used to annoy me. But over the years, with many iterations of the question, I've come to discern in it a certain cagey logic. After all, some projects succeed in spite of their systemic problems. They simply roll over unsolved issues through sheer force of will and energy, and bring the effort home to a successful conclusion. The What-if question, I now assume, is meant to steer discussion away from solving problems and focus it instead on the kind of enablers that can make problems not matter. Such enablers act by altering the dynamic of people working together. The leverage of such team effects can be enormous; an enabled project team can become unstoppable.

I've seen teams that were unstoppable, and probably you have, too. Such teams seem to "go nova," to use my colleague Tim Lister's phrase. What makes it happen? The short answer is that nothing *makes* it happen. You can't *make* unstoppable teams happen and neither can I. Sometimes they just do. It is a rare blend of good chemistry and good luck that lets the team gather momentum and then lets that momentum build on itself.

While there is no way to ensure this phenomenon, there are many ways to make it impossible. These are the different forms of "teamicide" that Tim and I discussed in our book, *Peopleware* [1]. Now if your project were plagued by one and only one kind of teamicide, routing it out might let the team take off. That would be the enabler. It wouldn't guarantee success—the team still might not jell for reasons of its own—but it would create a possibility of success that hadn't existed before.

The familiar "What if we only did one thing to improve?" question makes me reexamine my take on the organization to discover what such an enabler might be. About half the time, there is at least one avenue thus opened up that is worth investigating. And about half of those times, it's the same avenue. If you asked me to guess at something that might work in your own organization, I could pick this most frequently occurring enabler and offer it to you (without ever a look inside your shop), and feel we had one chance in four or better that it might help. "It wouldn't surprise me," I'd tell you, "to find that your people are frustrated by too much task switching. Take steps to let them work on one project only, one task at a time."

I'm always amazed by how many simultaneous tasks software developers are given. I run into people all the time who are assigned to one project but also working part-time on one or two others, and on call to do a bit of maintenance on the last program they completed, or sales support if the need arises. They zip off for five days of training, take one afternoon a week to organize the United Fund drive, and fill in for an hour each morning manning the customer support hot line. It's a wonder they don't go bonkers.

The human CPU is very inefficient at multi-tasking. We *seem* to switch gears well, but it's all an illusion. Of course, we don't let our inefficiency show. We don't betray the fact that task one, just interrupted, is still churning on in some corner of the brain, making it impossible to pay attention to the guy who is throwing tasks two and three at us. We smile and nod, not to look stupid. He goes away and we try to remember what task one was, but it's lost. And tasks two and three, well, they're floating tantalizingly in recent memory when the phone rings and task four comes spilling into the ear.

I make no pretense of knowing exactly how task switching works inside the brain. I have limited experience, and all of it with only this one brain. Maybe it's a defective unit. But my experience says that a complete switch of tasks involves some storing away of context for the interrupted task and loading of context for the new one. If the two contexts are completely different, this switch takes a good deal of time. While the switch is going on, the system is effectively down. It can't work constructively on either task. Once the new context is loaded, the brain is still in a torpid state, frustrated, maybe even a little angry. It takes time to come up to speed again. If there are enough switches in a short period of time, it never gets up to speed. The system is thrashing.

My rule of thumb is that three complete context switches use up a whole working day. That means context sets were stored and loaded that day, but no work was done.

Frustration and context switching are bad for team dynamics. Teams are an obsessive business. That means you and your teammates have to be allowed to be obsessively involved in one commonly owned subject area. Teams are never made up of part-timers. Oh, you try to make room for the occasional part-timer on a team because you'd so like for him or her to fit in, but it never really works. The sine qua non of team building is that each and every member has to be full-time on one and only one task, the task that defines the team. A group of split-responsibility, fragmented, and frustrated co-workers may be *called* a team, but they will never go nova.

Of course, frustration and context switching are bad for individual dynamics as well. So, multi-tasking assignments lead to poor individual efficiency and reduced possibility of positive team effects.

When I complain to managers that they've let their people become too fragmented, I get one of those looks we all got as children when we complained that bedtime came too early. They explain patiently to me that that's just the way it has to be. It's not their fault, they explain, that's how the real world is. But they're wrong. The real world is that fragmentation varies enormously from organization to organization. Two companies that are practically identical viewed from the outside will have drastically different degrees of fragmentation: one none, and the other way too much.

I've come to believe that fragmentation is due mostly to managerial sloppiness. It doesn't have to occur, and it won't if you take pains to stop it. If you only do one thing to improve, decrease the amount of task switching. You'll thus reduce frustration and waste, and make it possible for your teams to take off.

REFERENCE

[1]   T. DeMarco and T. Lister, *Peopleware: Productive Projects and Teams* (New York: Dorset House Publishing, 1987).

7

DESKTOP VIDEO: A TUTORIAL

Working with an overhead projector (OHP) all these years has made me keenly aware of the limitations of any static graphic. I would stare up sourly at a transparency I had just projected for my audience, thinking, "If only the damn thing could move, if only it could show a graph developing in front of the eye or a key element of a diagram exploding into its component parts or zooming into the portion I wanted to talk about next." But it couldn't.

One day I was so exasperated, I declared to myself that I'd never use an OHP again. (No halfway measures for this guy.) I went out and bought a ton of video equipment: decks and mixers and video boards and software to drive them and edit suites and animation controllers. Then I set out to make videos for use in my lectures as a kind of dynamic OHP. I would do the audio live, while the video showed my dancing graphics, exploding and developing and zooming and twirling and fragmenting and color-shifting and rocking and rolling to my heart's content.

I've since abandoned the scheme— trying to remember what gyration the video was about to do next used up so much of my brain power that I had none left to remember what I was going to say. All that's left of my grand experiment is the following essay.

7

DESKTOP VIDEO: A TUTORIAL

Desktop video is all the rage these days. You can't go to a computer show without bumping into someone with a huge screen showing an artful blend of live video with Macintosh®-generated graphics and text rolling over it or under it or dancing around it. In front of such a demo, you'll find your Video Honcho, chatting effortlessly about gen-locking and S-video and frame grabbers.

The purpose of this tutorial is to allow you to chat with such a fellow, without betraying the fact that you don't know what you're talking about. Of course, you could accomplish the same thing without reading the tutorial; you could do what I did and bring yourself to the brink of financial ruin by buying one of each of the myriad things you need to actually *do* desktop video. I will go into the costs a bit below, and you'll almost certainly see that reading the tutorial is going to be a far less costly solution for your needs.

PUTTING A GRAPHIC OUT TO VIDEO: THE PROBLEM
IN ABSTRACT

To begin, let's consider what's involved in putting a computer-generated graphic out to video, so you can record it on a VCR, for example. In the abstract, this is simple enough. Your Mac is already doing something very like what you'd like to accomplish: It's sending the graphic image out to your monitor. Once you get it to display exactly the graphic you want on the monitor screen, why can't you just shunt the image over to your VCR?

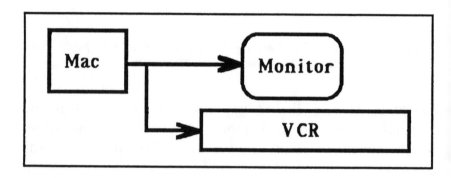

Figure I. Abstract view of what we'd like to do.

You might unplug the cable from the back of your monitor and plug it directly into the VCR. Of course, the obvious problem is that the cable connector doesn't fit into your VCR. That's no oversight, but reflects a long-standing and serious effort on the part of people who design video and computer equipment to thwart you in putting the two together.

Even if you could adapt the connector, it wouldn't help, since the protocol used to send an image to the monitor is incomprehensible and probably dangerous to your VCR. There are different numbers of conductors required, different voltage levels, different meanings assigned to the pins, and different information-encoding schemes.

Putting a computer-generated image out to video is, most of all, an exercise in format and protocol conversion. The standards of the computer industry and those of the video industry are utterly incompatible.

THE IMPORTANCE OF STANDARDS

Not only are the standards different between video and computing, but even within each of those disciplines, there is a multitude of standards. It seems that each of the two fields observed, very early, that standards were a good thing and so set out to develop as many as possible of them.

Mac computers and Sun and NeXT workstations, for example, all have slightly different ways to pass an image from processor to screen. When you add to that the baroque protocols of IBM and other similarly quaint architectures, it gets even worse.

If the variation of standards is bad in computing, it's even worse in video. The standards there are positively balkanized. Just to give you a taste: There are at least three ways to transmit a signal through the airwaves, six ways to write it onto a VHS cassette, five different formats of tape (varying in width, encoding scheme, and cassette geometry), three ways to pass it from source to monitor, and at least two dozen kinds of connectors and cables.

In the United States, Canada, and Mexico, we use a video protocol called NTSC, while in Europe they use PAL, and in Asia and South America there are others. Everything I shall write below is specifically relevant to NTSC as it is used in the State of Maine where I live. Some of it may apply elsewhere.

NTSC stands for Never the Same Color. This name derives from the fact that whatever color you put out into NTSC has been changed subtly into some other color by the time it gets displayed. The causes of this color variation are not precisely know, but are thought to include entropy and the Coriolis force.

There have been some recent and very interesting experiments conducted in California in which the entire NTSC transmission and all its associated gear were housed under a large crystal pyramid. Studies were then performed to see if the color variation was greater or less. The results have been inconclusive, except in what they imply about California.

SCREEN PAINTING

Screen painting had its origins in Japan in the eighth century. Here is one field where good old American ingenuity stole a march on the wily Japanese. The Japanese always painted on the *front* of the screen, and we were the ones who hit on the idea of using a transparent screen and painting on the back of it. The importance of this breakthrough is that you can then use electronic beams to paint the images. This has given us CRTs and VDUs (video display units) and television and Peewee Herman.

Of course, the problem of painting with electronic beams is that they then carry on through the screen and go into your head, resulting in a general softening of the noodle. Painting on the front of the screen didn't have this side effect. This is one explanation of the so-called Japanese Miracle, since the Japanese haven't got such a long history of having their noodles softened.

But that is a digression. I wanted to alert you to the drastically different screen painting methods used in video and computing. A computer paints its images

- in colored pixels
- laid down in rows from left to right and top to bottom
- scanned very rapidly, as fast as 72 Hz

On the other hand, a TV paints an image differently:

- in *lines*, analog strips of color drawn from left to right
- interlaced, so that all the odd-numbered lines are laid down first, and then the even-numbered lines
- at relatively slow scan rates, such as 30 frames per second in NTSC

Finally, the line height is not exactly the same as the pixel height, and the aspect ratio of the TV screen is different from that of most computer screens.

ENTER THE GEN-LOCK CIRCUIT

A gen-lock circuit or gen-lock card does part of the conversion needed to translate from computer image to video. It takes the digital array in the bit map and converts it into an analog signal, arbitrates between pixel and line height, slows down the scan, and interlaces odd and even lines. It also crops off those portions of the computer image that won't fit. On the input side, it does analog-to-digital conversion, line-to-pixel resolution in the opposite direction, de-interlaces and recrops or distorts to fit the different frame. Finally, at least some gen-lock cards do chroma-keying to superimpose computerized images on live video. Because it does all these totally unrelated things, the device is called a gen-lock. I hope this is clear.

A typical gen-lock plugs into your Mac as a nu-bus card. It presents itself as a second (or nth) video card. The signal it puts out is Neither Fish Nor Fowl, or NFNF. It has TV-style scan rate, interlacing, line forms, and a television aspect ratio, but it is still transmitted in computer protocol over an R-G-B-plus-Sync cable. That means the red, green, and blue information are passed separately and the timing information (to help the display figure out where the top of the frame is) is in its own conductor. Your normal Mac monitor can't display this signal, nor can your TV. But a multi-sync monitor is very forgiving about varying rates and formats, so it can display this signal.

THE FORMAT CONVERTER

The next thing you need (each one of these things costs a fortune, by the way) is a format converter. The format converter converts what you've got (RGB+S) into what you want: a signal format that can be understood by video equipment. Actually, you need two format converters: a decoder for outgoing signals and an encoder for incoming signals. Or maybe it's the other way around.

What is the format needed to get the signal that last step to your VCR? There are three choices. The oldest is what is called RF, for Radio Frequency. The RF format is an analog mixture of color, light, amplitude, timing, and audio information, pretty much the way they come in from your antenna. RF signals are carried over coaxial cables with big, clunky F-connectors on their ends. The F-connector is the one with the little needle in the middle. All cable boxes, all VCRs, and all but the oldest TVs can work with RF signals.

The second possibility is *composite* format. A composite signal is carried over simple shielded cables with RCA connectors. These are called "video dubbing cables." You need one for the video and one for the audio. I guess the one for the audio might be called a video audio dubbing cable. Sometimes you need two dubbing cables for the audio, since there are increasingly two audio tracks on a video tape, and sometimes there are three.

The newest equipment can accept a signal in the third format, called S-video. S-video, or separated video, is what is written onto an S-VHS cassette. The cable for an S-video signal has a small round connector at each end with five or six pins inside it. I have never found anyone who could say for sure how many pins there are because S-video equipment is very expensive and people who are old enough to be able to afford it can't see very well.

WHAT IS THIS S-VIDEO, ANYWAY?

S-video is a transmission protocol in which luminance and chrominance are separately encoded. I have been actively involved in desktop video for more than two years now, and probably two-hundred people have told me during that time that S-video is a protocol with separately encoded luminance and chrominance. It took me a long time to realize that none of them had any idea of what that meant. I don't have any idea of what it means either, and you certainly aren't going to learn what it means from this tutorial. But don't dismay. Remember, our goal was not to master the concepts, but only to appear to have mastered them. People who are into DTV talk glibly about separately encoded luminance and chrominance, and you will have to learn to do that, too.

Practice saying the following sentence:

> The importance of separately encoded luminance and chrominance cannot be overstated.

Excellent. Say it with assurance and, if people look like they may be about to ask you for definitions, change the subject quickly (to gen-locking, for example).

Those who are real video cognoscenti refer to luminance and chrominance by their more familiar names of Y and C. C stands for chrominance, and Y for, um, luminance. Or possibly not. Don't worry about it.

Practice saying the following sentences:

> Keep the ole Y and C separate. That's the ticket!

There, you're making splendid progress.

QUICK SUMMARY OF THE THREE VIDEO SIGNAL PROTOCOLS

I want to take you one more time through the three signal and cabling protocols, just to make sure you've got them right.

1. The RF signal: an analog mix of video and audio signals, carried over coaxial cable with F-connectors on both ends. Although it is a composite of audio and video, it's not called composite, since that name is reserved for:

2. The composite signal: separated audio and video carried over two or three dubbing cables with RCA jacks on both ends. Although it has video separate from audio, it's not called separate video, since that term is reserved for:

3. The S-video signal: separately encoded luminance and chrominance, carried over a thin (enormously expensive) cable with S-jacks at each end.

I am not making this up.

Where were we? Oh, yes. The format converter gives you one of these three signals, and you can plug it directly into your deck. In the opposite direction, the signal goes from the deck to the converter (in one of the three signal protocols), out the converter in RGB+S interlaced, underscanned, slow refresh, analog, and into the gen-lock card where it gets converted to digital. The final configuration is shown in Fig. 2.

A WORD ABOUT COST

You might think from what you've read so far that the dominant characteristic of desktop video is baffling terminology, or perhaps abstruse protocols and formats. You couldn't be more wrong. The dominant characteristic of desktop video is sticker shock. Only people with a long history of looking at beachfront real estate are really ready to confront the costs of desktop video.

It's not just the cost of each component that kills you, but the sheer number of things you need. In my modest setup, I have 2 nu-bus cards, 2 format converters, 2 new decks, 2 monitors, a new camera (the old one wasn't S-video and, of course, the importance of separately encoded luminance and chrominance cannot be overstated), a mixer, a switch box, 24 cables, 9 cable adapters, 2 new microphones, and 19 new software packages. That doesn't count lights, cassettes, or the new tie I had to buy because the old one flickered on an interlaced display.

I made up a spreadsheet with all of the various components and the price I actually paid for each one. I am not going to show you those exact prices because to do so would be very unprofessional. The prices of all these items are discounted in a seemingly random fashion by organizations all over the country. If I gave you the precise price that I paid for the Macro-Mind Accelerator, for example, or the NuVista card, I would expose myself to being giggled at by people wherever I went who had gotten the same thing for half the price.

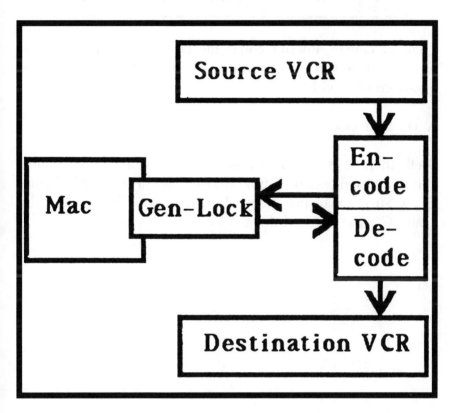

Figure 2. Desktop video configuration.

Anyone who recognized me at a conference would come up and poke an elbow in my ribs and say, "DeMarco, you turkey, you should have shopped around." Being poked in the ribs and having people giggle at you behind their hands is the essence of unprofessionalism.

While I am not willing to share with you the detailed prices I paid for each item, I will show you the bottom line, the very last cell of my spreadsheet where the total prints out:

55			
56			
57	GRAND TOTAL	***OVERFLOW***	
58			
59			

That, of course, doesn't count the cost of your time. Figure more or less forty-five minutes of effort for each finished nanosecond of video.

A JOB WELL DONE

Well, there it is. You've learned all you really need to know about desktop video. Enjoy yourself at the next MacWorld Expo. Stroll up to the Video Honcho and tell him to keep his Y and C separate.

8

NONTECHNOLOGICAL ISSUES IN SOFTWARE ENGINEERING

This short position paper begins with the story of my conversion from a technology-can-conquer-all kind of developer to one who has an inkling at least that there are sociological issues that matter. It goes on to show where this inkling has led.

8

NONTECHNOLOGICAL ISSUES
IN SOFTWARE ENGINEERING

During a panel at the 5th International Conference on Software Engineering in San Diego in 1981, Fred Brooks told a story that has stayed with me ever since. He said he'd been running the same project over and over again as part of his laboratory course on software development at the University of North Carolina. Each of the projects had the same deliverable, same schedule, and same team size. What varied from semester to semester were the methods and techniques used. But, he reflected, methods and techniques didn't seem to matter as much as he'd expected. They didn't matter nearly as much as certain nontechnological factors like team harmony, clever role allocation, and group sense of purpose. The very best technology never had as much impact as girlfriend or boyfriend trouble.

In the years since, I've found that most managers readily accept Brooks's premise. They know, for example, that the project's *sociology* will be more important to eventual success or failure than the project's *technology*. But they don't run their projects accordingly. In particular, they don't dedicate their time and energies at all according to their professed belief about the priorities. They focus all their attention on technology and virtually none on sociology.

THE "I HATE POLITICS" MANAGER

If sociology is more important to project success than technology, then a manager has to be principally involved in managing the project's sociology. She or he needs to spend the most time and energy on tasks like team formation and jell, role assignment, hiring, motivation, bureaucracy reduction, workplace redesign and tuning, and environmental improvement.

Such tasks lead one into the "soft" domains of personality, individual skills and talents, and corporate power division. This is scary stuff. A young manager may well be daunted at the notion of taking on the dreaded Space and Services establishment, for example, to get the project a much-needed conference room or even an extra table or whiteboard. So what happens? He (only the male of the species is this dumb) writes down "Talk to Space and Services!" on a little piece of paper, throws it into the wastebasket, and convokes a nine-day meeting to select a new 4GL. Result:

Technology: 1
Sociology: 0

The evident reason for this is that the manager knows how to do technology, but not how to do sociology. He or she doesn't know how to manage.

If only we could come to grips with this problem, the solution would not be far behind. But we don't come to grips with it at all. We deny. The most common form of denial is to lump all the soft, people-oriented kinds of management into the category *politics*, and then take refuge in the heroic "I hate politics" defense. I can think of no field in which politics is viewed with more distaste than in software. We use this distaste to explain away the dictates of learning to be real managers.

Politics is a noble science. It is, according to no less an authority than Aristotle, one of the five branches of philosophy. Along with the others (metaphysics, epistemology, ethics, and aesthetics), politics is not intrinsically evil; rather, it is part of the process of understanding and doing good. It is indispensable for doing good as a manager.

To take aim squarely at our most important managerial failings, we need to rehabilitate politics as a noble science, admit frankly that we aren't good at it yet, and get on with the necessary business of becoming good at it.

LETTING TEAMS HAPPEN

One particular aspect of project sociology requires special attention here: the role of the team. Teams happen all the time in project work; when they do, they are judged by most participants to be a major benefit. By that, I mean they benefit the project (work gets done more effectively), and they benefit the team members (work is more fun). If you've ever worked on a jelled team, you probably already know how important it can be.

The maddening thing about teams is that they happen by themselves but it is difficult or impossible to *make* them happen. Failure to force teams to form is due, I believe, to managers trying to set up teams with themselves as leaders. That sounds like a good idea, but it isn't. I am more and more convinced that those who talk most about leadership have the most difficulty forming meaningfully jelled teams. The reason is that jelled teams aren't really led. They are networks, not hierarchies. All members are virtual peers. The leadership function is distributed, that is, different members take control at different times.

In my own experience as a manager, I went through four stages of team awareness. I will share them with you in the hope that you may be able to avoid the first three.

- ☐ Stage one was Hysterical Optimism: "I will form this team around myself by force of pure personal dynamism."
- ☐ Stage two was Bitter Disillusionment: "These turkeys just don't want to work as a team."

☐ Stage three was Defensive Retrenchment: "Teams are uppity and threatening anyway, so I won't let them happen even if they are inclined to."

☐ Finally, stage four was Acceptance: "Teams are uppity and threatening, but wonderful nonetheless; I will thank my lucky stars if my staff jells into a workable team."

REPRISE

My colleague Tim Lister illustrates the sociology/technology dichotomy with the following observation: Imagine your boss just plunked a specification on your desk and asked, "How long will it take you and one other person to get this job done?" What's the first question out of your mouth?

Would you ask, "Can we use object-oriented methods?" or "What CASE system can we buy?" or "Is it okay to use rapid prototyping?" Of course not. Your first question is,

Who is the other person?

Congratulations! You've just elevated the sociological above the technological. But don't forget to carry on. It's not just thing number one that needs to be concerned with project sociology; it's also things two through two hundred.

9

CHALLENGE OF THE '90s:
THE SCHOOLS

Bruce Taylor, my editor at the journal *Human Capital,* asked me in early 1990 to undertake a series of reviews and opinion pieces about the state of public education in America. At the time, I was an outsider, but not a complete outsider. Bruce and I had together founded a small nonprofit organization the year before called the Penobscot Compact, and registered it under the Maine State Aspirations Program. The purpose of the Compact was to focus the energies and resources of corporations in mid-coast Maine to help the public schools. Our particular approach was what we called the Partnership Program: Companies allowed their employees to become partnered with teachers in the school system and freed them for up to three hours a week to work in the schools. Their time was the contribution of the corporation. Their passion and energy and caring was their own contribution.

As a side effect of running the Compact during its first years, I spent many hours in the schools, scouting potential partnerships. I ended up working in every grade level from kindergarten to the last year of high school, and meeting literally hundreds of teachers.

When *IEEE Software* invited me to submit a paper for their Challenges of the '90s issue, I decided to write about the schools. I tried to persuade the readers that bailing out schools was not just a challenge in general, but was *our* challenge—that helping kids achieve their potential was, in some sense, the ultimate software project.

9

CHALLENGE OF THE '90s: THE SCHOOLS

Copyright © 1990 IEEE. Reprinted, with permission, from *IEEE Software*, November 1990.

The word *challenge* has a near religious significance to software developers. It is the presence of challenge that gives meaning to our work, that separates broadening experience from the merely humdrum.

We apply our creativity almost as much to finding challenge as to meeting it. So, the most prosaic assignment might be embellished by the developer with an extra need for elegance, or tightness, or spareness, or speed, or flexibility even beyond the stated requirement. As a young manager, I was exasperated by these embellishments. I would explain endlessly to my developers that the routing module didn't have to be *so* fast, or that the display program didn't have to use the *very latest* object/encapsulation techniques. I felt they were adding irresponsibly to the requirement just to increase the amusement value of the work. I now believe they were reconstruing their assignments to find challenge where there would otherwise have been none.

The need to find challenge, even by adding to a requirement, is admirable enough. If the embellishment is sufficiently artificial, we must begin wondering at the absence of a more natural source of challenge. We can do a job with one hand tied behind our back (thus making the work more nearly equal to the worker), but after a while, why bother? This is the state I believe we have come to in software today.

As I consider the technological challenges we might pose ourselves over the next decade, they all strike me as somewhat artificial. Yes, we will be able to master some of these new technologies—that will certainly be an amusing enough endeavor—but what shall we then use them for? Will it just be to do and redo more of the same work we have done over the last thirty years?

THE JOB WE BEGAN IN THE 1960S IS NOW MOSTLY DONE

In the decade of the 1960s, we set out to automate industry and government, beginning in the central offices. In the 1970s, we carried automation to the line operations, and reworked many of the first-generation batch systems to run on-line. In the 1980s, we redid much of our earlier work to take advantage of distributed processing. I know this is the kind of observation we self-proclaimed experts often live to regret, but here it is anyway: I think the job of automating the business world is now mostly done.

There may still be two million or more of us employed in industry, but most will not be much involved with anything significantly new. Consider:

- ☐ A third to half the programming population is occupied maintaining and enhancing old code. This fact is often cited as a failure of our design methods, but it might equally well be viewed as an overall success in achieving our initial mission: Successful automation is bound to increase the proportion of existing code to new.

- ☐ We have long used five-to-eight years as an expected average lifetime of software, but today that figure seems pessimistic. One of my client companies, for example, has more than eighteen million lines of code that are seventeen years old or older.

- ☐ The much-discussed software backlog is beginning to look like a fiction. The projects on last year's backlog show up again on this year's backlog, passed over by many more essential pieces of work. The backlog may be nothing more than a list of nice-to-have-someday software that hasn't got the usefulness to offset its likely cost.

☐ Cost/benefit analysis is now, for the most part, just cost analysis. A new development project that offers specific, *measurable* benefit numbers is a rarity. (Is it possible we've already done all the projects that have obvious, tangible benefits?)

☐ The market for software people has softened, particularly in the U.S., over the past 2 years. Weakness in the entry market has begun to discourage students from studying computer science. Only 3.2 percent of college freshmen today are majoring in computer science, compared to 8.6 percent in 1980.

Using better technology to redo and enhance old systems may be a sufficient challenge for many individual software workers, but for a challenge big enough for our entire industry, I believe, we need to look beyond the business world. It is not so much new methods, but new domains that will challenge us. There is no new domain I can think of that is more promising than the schools.

EDUCATING YOUNG PEOPLE IS THE ULTIMATE
SOFTWARE PROJECT

An essential activity of any software project—helping a user understand and learn how to make use of a new system—is also the most essential activity of the schools. The difference is that in industry, the user is a business person and the system is WYZBANG-4 (or whatever), while in the schools, the user is a young person and the system is English, or math, or science. Software professionals have skills that are specifically relevant to the education of our young people: human communication skills, systemization and automation skills, and training skills.

Part of our community's involvement in the schools is readily apparent. The educational software industry is today on the order of $128 million* and growing. Projects at Apple and IBM (and probably elsewhere) have set out to design an integrated classroom computer, which can be expected to further fuel the educational software segment. Alan Kay's Vivarium project at the Los Angeles Open School, for example, has built a small Dynabook variant directly into the primary school desk to make computing an integral part of the learning process. Computers so woven into the fabric of a classroom are likely to become available and perhaps even ubiquitous during the 1990s. The move toward a classroom computer could be accelerated by a trans-corporate organization, similar to the Open Systems Foundation, to derive a single architecture with opportunities for multiple vendors to supply components. (See [1] for such a proposal.) Even in the absence of trans-corporate efforts, integrated computing in the schools and a growing educational software segment will likely be a characteristic of this decade.

For those of us who are not building educational software, there are opportunities as well to lend support to the schools. This involvement is only indirectly tied to the for-profit orientation of our employers. Nonetheless, software organizations today are contributing their skills and valued human resources more and more heavily to the schools. As Peter Drucker points out, the United States economy is currently contributing some $15 billion a year of professional labor [2], a significant part of it to the schools.

THE WAY THINGS ARE AND THE WAY THEY COULD BE

Pulitzer Prize-winning author Tracy Kidder took as a recent project to write something that would help his fellow citizens understand the dilemma of the American schools. Kidder chose a

---

*Data for 1989 from the Software Publishers Association, Washington, D.C. This figure includes instructional software only, not business software sold to the schools nor Integrated Learning Systems.

method that was direct and characteristic: He sat in the back of a fifth-grade class for an entire school year and then wrote a book about what he observed. The result is *Among Schoolchildren* [3].

Reading this book is an upsetting and emotional experience. You meet a teacher, a principal, a few parents, and a room full of fifth-graders from the Kelly School in Holyoke, Mass. You come to know them in some detail. They are all real people. The teacher, Mrs. Christine Zajac, is as admirable a public servant as you can imagine. She is competent, learned, and passionate. She is just the kind of teacher you wanted all your own school years and loved if you happened to have her. She is the kind of teacher you wish could be assigned to your kids all the way through school. Her students are crazy about her. That's the good news. The bad news is this woman is failing. Her fifth-graders, some of them at least, are going to become the kind of awful statistic we see so often in the papers: young adults who can't make change, who can't write a coherent sentence, who can't remember where Paraguay is, or who think the esophagus is a Greek tragedy.

As part of my current involvement, I have been sitting in the back of schoolrooms myself over the past year. I have observed classes from first grade through high school, and even found a few Chris Zajacs of my own. And, I am convinced, these excellent teachers are failing too. I'll go into some of the reasons below, but first I shall put my own solution down in black and white and propose it to you in the form of a challenge:

> We have to step in and help get the schools going again.

By "we," I don't mean "we humans" or "we Americans." If you read the challenge that way, you might agree with it, but conclude with a grateful sigh that it applies to someone else. I mean specifically "we software engineers." What I really mean is you and me.

In the sections below, I point out some exciting ways the software community has already begun to play an active role in the schools, and I present a game plan for how others of us can take part. First, I'll need to deal with two Easy Outs, observations we might like to use to let ourselves off the hook.

Easy Out Number One

This is not *our* problem. Someone certainly ought to take on the challenge of the schools' crisis. But shouldn't that someone really be the government, or the state, or the schools themselves?

We are part of a global economy. We are going to become an increasingly irrelevant part unless we solve the problem of the schools. (I won't try to prove that to you because I think you know it already.) Expecting this problem to be solved by government and the schools' establishment is a perfect example of Jerry Weinberg's First Law of Bad Management: "When something isn't working, do more of it." [4]

As we watch the unraveling of centrally planned systems in Eastern Europe, we have to stop cheering long enough to think about the implications for our own centrally planned education system. It implies we have to bring private enterprise to bear on the problem in a partnership of education and business. Businesses that don't invest in their future work force won't be able to find a future work force to keep them competitive. What businesses have to invest is not just money, but skilled resources: communicators, systems builders, and trainers.

Since you and your organization have skills that could help in the present crisis, I appeal to you in the same way I would appeal to doctors and nurses if the crisis were an earthquake.

> **Easy Out Number Two**
>
> The problem of the schools could be solved without any help from us. If they would only get back to basics and forget the dumb fads (whole language reading, open classroom, new math, and so on), we'd have schools as good as ever.

Forget the simple solutions. Fads are not the problem. Teachers and administrators are not the problem. Even stingy investment is not, by itself, the problem. Children today have needs that aren't met by traditional schooling. The schools are being asked to take on an increasing part of the parents' role. Beyond their original charter, they now need to deal with single-parent homes, two-job families, and latchkey children.

The so-called crisis of the schools is really a crisis of society, one whose burden falls squarely on our children. The report from the President's Commission on Excellence in Education [5] signaled this fact with a sobering statistic: By the time the average young person leaves high school, he or she has spent 3,200 hours interacting with one or both parents, 12,000 hours in the schools, and 18,000 hours watching television. (Maybe we ought to replace our War on Drugs with a War on Television.) The inevitable result is children who are more passive, less confident, less articulate, and far more needy of special attention than in generations past.

If we can move past the illusion of simple solutions, then we can get on with the business of implementing some very hard ones. The hard solutions involve a lot more adults taking part in the educational process. Unfortunately, since the schools will be unable to pay for this increased participation, the solution will have to be part of the investment that companies and organizations make in their own future human capital.

A CHALLENGE, NOT A PIPE DREAM

I am not encouraging you to go where no one has gone before. Presented below are brief descriptions of what some of your colleagues are already doing. I've chosen some large and ambitious examples and others considerably more modest.

✓ Apple Computer has more than fifty professional employees whose time is contributed for a few hours each week to the local Nimitz School to tutor elementary school youngsters in reading, writing, and math.

✓ Ex-Johnson & Johnson systems analyst Sue Blake has begun a "floating classroom" program. With a mix of private and public funds, she has put together a marine biology sequence on board the two-masted schooner *Flying Fish*. She sails each week, fall and spring, with six to ten public school students. They are at sea for three days at a time to study marine wildlife in situ. Public schools of Islesboro, Maine, participate in her program.

✓ Dustin Heuston (principal of WICAT Systems) has organized an experimental school in Sandy, Utah, to investigate the use of computerized learning laboratories. Children in the laboratories work on-line forty-five minutes a day. He is also helping install such laboratories in disadvantaged schools in New York's South Bronx.

✓ IBM, through its faculty loan program, has placed approximately a thousand of its employees in some two hundred schools attended by minority or disabled students. The on-loan employees (still on the IBM payroll and receiving full benefits) serve full-time in teaching and administrative capacities in the schools.

✓ Project "Stretch Beyond" in the Kennebunk area of southern Maine has extended the school day with a series of twenty

afternoon classes (in remedial reading, languages, computing, and science projects, for example), taught by knowledge
workers from the community and attended voluntarily by
more than two hundred children.

✓ Our own Penobscot Compact has fifteen local employers
who contribute the paid time of their knowledge workers
to tutor students one-on-one in public school classrooms.
The Compact has a training program to help new teacher's
assistants be useful and smoothly coordinated with the
teacher who manages each class.

✓ The Business Roundtable publishes a directory of companies
participating in its education task force partnerships program [6]. Conspicuous in the directory are major players
in the field of software and computing (AT&T, BellSouth,
Boeing, Control Data, DEC, Disney, Eastman Kodak, GE,
GTE, Hewlett-Packard, Honeywell, IBM, ITT, NCR,
NYNEX, Pacific Telesis, Southern California Edison, Southern Company, Southwestern Bell, Texas Instruments, 3M,
Time, TRW, UNISYS, and Xerox, plus most of the large
banks and insurance companies).

A GAME PLAN FOR INVOLVEMENT IN THE SCHOOLS

A convenient vehicle for participation in the schools is the
business-education compact. As a result of the President's Summit
on Education (held at the University of Virginia, September 27-
28, 1989), the then-governors of all fifty states committed to
foster such compacts. The Department of Education of your state
government will tell you how to make contact with your local
compact, or how to form one if there isn't one yet. I urge you
to get involved.

Here is the ticklish part: Try to get your company involved,
too. For the Penobscot Compact, I've been getting companies
to contribute their salaried employees for three hours or more
per week for a whole school term to work in the schools, plus

some additional time for training. All it has taken is asking. To my surprise, business people everywhere are fully aware that remaining competitive in the global marketplace will require substantial new investment in K-12 education, and they're aware that the companies they manage are going to have to do their part. This is a rare moment when the iron is hot and ready to be struck, and everyone knows it.

Of course, your boss might look at you as if you just arrived from some other planet. She or he might write you off forever after as a kook, a nonprofessional, and a danger to the sacred schedule. But then, this wouldn't be a challenge, would it, if there weren't a real possibility of failure.

As to what your organization ought to do, I propose a two-part plan. The easier of the two parts is to lend some assistance in the computerization of the schools. Schools everywhere believe that more computers and software are a key element of their own transformation. There probably aren't enough computers, but knowledge of how to plug them together and get them working is in even shorter supply. In the local middle school library of my town, for example, there is one PC/XT® that hadn't been used for weeks because of a missing RS-232C cable. The librarian had simply no idea of how to go about ordering a replacement cable. She shouldn't have to know about such things—this is a woman who knows the name of every single child in the school, and knows (better than the children themselves) who has read what and whether they liked it or not. *We* know how to get such systems up and running, so *we* have to pitch in and do it.

At another school library not too far away from my home-town, there is a modem that was intended to connect students to MaineCat, a centralized library access service of the State University. That wasn't in use either, not because of cabling but because of a bureaucratic problem: The school's budgeting process had trouble with an open-ended commitment such as long-distance access time. So the system wasn't being used. Such an obstacle can be almost insurmountable in a governmental bureaucracy. But in our town, there are literally scores of business executives able and willing to say, "For goodness sake, get the phone company to send that bill to me; I'll set it up to be paid every month along with our own phone bills and we'll never again have to worry about seeing it on the school's budget." End of problem.

What can you do to get more computers in the schools, particularly given that the schools are not going to be able to pay for the ones they need? There must be millions of aging PCs in industry that are about to be replaced and that could be contributed to the schools. Such machines might already be depreciated entirely, so they could be passed on to the schools without even a bookkeeping entry. To confirm this notion, I called the National Bureau of Facts (also known as Capers Jones). He told me there were more than four million older Macs, and 8088- and 80286-based PCs in that category [7]. If your company has small machines about to be retired, arrange for them to be contributed to your local compact, or contact the Computer Clearinghouse, run by the Penobscot Compact [8] to make sure they end up in school classrooms.

The second half of the game plan is to introduce salaried knowledge workers (their time contributed by the businesses that employ them) into the schools as individual tutors, teaching assistants, and aides. This has to be done in a gentle, non-threatening manner and the resources you provide will be managed by the teachers so they can better achieve their own lesson plans on their own schedules.

REPRISE

Like the nurse or paramedic who comes skidding to a stop on the highway and runs back to give aid at the scene of an accident, we systems and software people are taking on the challenge of the schools. It is not guilt that propels us, but the satisfaction of having skills and knowledge that *could* be critical. This is not somebody else's problem; it is ours.

It's bucket brigade time for the schools. I've tried to persuade you that you have the ideal set of talents to help out, but even if you're not entirely convinced of that, I hope you'll pitch in and carry a bucket anyway.

To end, I return to the story of Mrs. Zajac, the teacher who is at the center of *Among Schoolchildren*. As she looks back on her thirteen years on the front line of the schools, she shares a sad observation with Tracy Kidder, the author. I had to read it a few times before its full meaning sunk in, as though my mind were unwilling to accept such a distressing thought:

> *She found it hard enough after thirteen years to believe that all fifth-graders' futures lay before them out of sight, and not in plain view behind.*

The challenge is there in her words: Let's do whatever we must do to put our children's futures right in front of them, where children's futures belong.

REFERENCES

[1]   T. DeMarco, "Computing in the Schools: Turning Down the Glitz," *Human Capital*, July 1990.

[2]   P. Drucker, *The New Realities* (New York: Harper & Row, 1989).

[3]   T. Kidder, *Among Schoolchildren* (Boston: Houghton Mifflin, 1989).

[4]   G.M. Weinberg, *Quality Software Management, Vol. 1: Systems Thinking* (New York: Dorset House Publishing, 1992).

[5]   *A Nation at Risk*, U.S. Government Printing Office (Washington, D.C.: 1983).

[6]   *Business Means Business About Education*, The Business Roundtable (New York: June 1989).

[7]   C. Jones, private correspondence, January 1990.

[8]   Penobscot Compact, Inc., P.O. Box 160, Camden, ME 04843.

10

SOFTWARE DEVELOPMENT: STATE OF THE ART VS. STATE OF THE PRACTICE

In 1985, Tim Lister and I wrote a paper entitled "Programmer Performance and the Effects of the Workplace," and presented it to the 8th International Conference on Software Engineering in London. It was our first public statement about the Coding War Games, a series of benchmarking exercises that Tim and I had been running for several years. By the time we were done running annual coding wars, we had a unique body of evidence, far more than we had been able to analyze for the 1985 paper. In fact, we had submissions from more than 700 programmers who had all undertaken to write and test a piece of code to exactly the same specification. To this day, I don't think there has ever been a larger programming benchmarking exercise performed.

It seemed a shame to throw the submissions away, but we knew they'd have to go soon, as the weight of those hundreds of listings, dumps, traces, test results, and filled-out forms was beginning to cause permanent sag in the floors of our Guild Hall. Before that drastic step, we decided to delve into the data one more time and report on what new conclusions could be drawn. The result was our second coauthored ICSE paper, presented in Pittsburgh on May 16, 1989.

10

SOFTWARE DEVELOPMENT:
STATE OF THE ART VS. STATE OF THE PRACTICE

with Tim Lister, The Atlantic Systems Guild

The state of the art of software development has changed considerably from the folkloric approaches of the 1950s and 1960s. But has the state of the practice kept up? A commonly held (rather cynical) view is that the great revolutions associated with the names of Dijkstra, Hoare, Mills, Myers, Parnas, Wirth, and others might as well not have happened for all the effect they had on the practice of the average developer.

During the period 1984 through 1987, we conducted a series of performance benchmarking exercises to allow individuals and organizations to evaluate their relative productivity. The emphasis of the benchmarks was on speed of program construction and low defect rate. A side effect of the exercise was that nearly 400 programmers wrote the same program (they all wrote to the same specification) and sent in listings of these programs along with their questionnaires, time logs, and test results. This afforded us an opportunity to assess the design and coding practices of a wide sample of developers.

1. BACKGROUND

Both individuals and the organizations they work for are aware of a distressing ignorance of how their effectiveness compares to that of their peers and competitors. Beginning in 1984, we offered both of these groups the opportunity to take part in a kind of "implementation bake-off" called the Coding War Games to help them assess their relative productivity. These exercises were run according to the following rules:

☐ Developers took part in pairs; the two individuals of each pair competed with each other as well as with other pairs in the exercise.

☐ All participants wrote the same program to the same specification.

☐ After design, coding, desk-check, and compilation, pair members exchanged programs for testing; development was thus conducted using a cleanroom approach, as described in [1]; programs were not repaired at any point.

☐ Defects reported included all the defects present at the end of desk-check.

☐ After their own tests, developers ran our predefined tests on the product.

☐ Submissions sent to us were identified by a code number drawn by the individual at the beginning of the exercise; only the individual knew his or her code; results were conveyed back to participants by code number, thus assuring confidentiality.

(A summary of findings from the 1984 and 1985 Coding War Games is presented in [2].)

Over the period of the experiment, we had 392 individuals take part in the coding wars. Participants came from 79 organizations. We divided the participants by language used into 7 communities. The relative proportions by language are shown in Fig. 1.

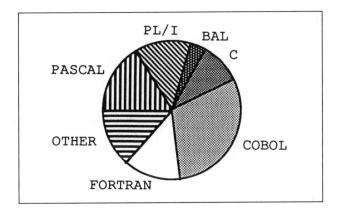

Figure I. Participants by language community.

There were 118 COBOL programmers, and 50 in the group called "Other." Included under "Other" were Ada, Modula-2, Forth, Cybil, Mapper, MUMPS, Jovial, APL, and some languages that we couldn't identify at all.

A biasing characteristic of our sample is that the participants were curious about how good they were. In addition, the participants were solicited through announcements in various journals and through seminars and conferences, thus proving that they could read or worked for organizations with nonzero training and travel budgets. Aside from these admitted biases, the sample seemed normal to us. Individuals came from all kinds of organizations: financial, service, engineering, academic, and the public sector. There were participants from the U.S., the United Kingdom, and Denmark. They were all professional programmers, ranging in experience from one to sixteen years.

To determine if the improved state of the art of software development is indeed reflected in the practice, we examined the listings submitted by language. We counted executable statements and declarations, modules, subroutine invocations, pathological connections, module size, variable locality, and coupling. In addition, we attempted to assess module binding strength. Not all analyses were performed on all language groups.

2. HYPOTHESES TO TEST

We selected seven indications of good modularization and programming technique, as reflected in the literature. We formulated each of these into a positive hypothesis, asserting that the technique was reflected in practice. We then analyzed participants' code to confirm or refute each hypothesis.

The seven hypotheses were

1. Developers divide programs into modules of manageable size.
2. Developers attempt to maximize locality of data.
3. Developers attempt to maximize module binding strength.
4. Developers attempt to practice data hiding.
5. Developers can use cleanroom methods to develop zero-defect products.
6. Developers practice structured coding.
7. Organizations with strongly enforced design methodologies achieve meaningful convergence of design from individual to individual.

3. THE RESULTS: AN ASSESSMENT OF THE STATE OF THE PRACTICE

It is possible that the task of wading through 300+ listings of the same program causes severe damage to the human judgmental capacities. If that isn't the explanation, then we must conclude that the state of modularization and programming technique is surprisingly respectable. This is exactly the opposite of what we expected to find. Based on an initial scan of a subset of the data, we were convinced we would be writing a paper demonstrating that the state of the practice was utterly uninfluenced by the state of the art. (Such a paper might have been more amusing.) Five of the seven hypotheses were confirmed. The details are presented below:

Hypothesis 1 (use of small modules): Confirmed

In all of the following, we use the word *module* to mean a closed subroutine with a single identifier by which the unit can be activated as a whole. By the middle 1970s, the case for small modules was already being made persuasively in the literature (see [3, 4], for example). But hearsay evidence implied that the state of the practice even 10 years later was a module of 500 lines or more. This is complicated by an early "modularization" act performed by the manager at the time of job assignment. These allocations are usually of at least 500 lines, and are also called modules. But do developers then implement these as undivided monoliths, or subdivide them further, out of respect for the principle of small modules?

Our sample indicated a strong preference for subdivision into small modules. The average module was 23 statements. In an analysis of 200 COBOL and Pascal programs, we found only 55 that had even a single module that exceeded a page of listing (the limit proposed by Mills).

Use of small modules paid off handsomely. When we analyzed the records of those 55 developers who allowed (one or more) large modules, we found that they had been substantially outdone by those who exhibited a more serious respect for small modules. The no-large-module subset had 38 percent fewer defects and was nearly twice as likely to pass the aggregate test of functionality (referred to below as the *acid test*) included in our test set. When we divided the sample into quartiles based on speed and accuracy, we found an increasing number of long-module users in the poorer performing quartiles:

Performers in	
1st quartile	21% had long module(s)
2nd quartile	31% had long module(s)
3rd quartile	36% had long module(s)
4th quartile	47% had long module(s)

Hypothesis 2 (maximum locality): Partially confirmed

Locality analysis was performed only on the Pascal subset. As a coarse metric of locality, we looked at the percentage of all variables that were defined so as to be visible in only one module. (The metric is coarse because variables that are truly local to the main-line module are nonetheless visible to subordinate modules under the scoping rules of Pascal.) We defined a *locality factor* as the count of local variables divided by the count of all variables. Locality factors varied from 0 (all variables visible to all modules) to .96 (only 4 percent of variables visible outside of the defining module). The average locality was .51. Only 12 percent of the sample had a locality factor of less than .20. Developers were clearly making an effort to keep as many variables as possible local to their defining modules.

Emphasis on high locality paid off: 1st quartile performers had average locality factors nearly 25 percent higher than 4th quartile performers. The subset of programs with higher-than-median locality had 63 percent fewer errors than programs with lower than median locality.

Hypothesis 3 (strong module binding): Confirmed

The idea that a module ought to be strongly connected within and loosely connected to its exterior comes to us from [4, 5, 6]. The tightness of connection within is called *binding strength*. Most writers on the subject describe functional binding (all elements of the module act to achieve a single function) as the strongest.

There was one algorithm in the benchmark problem that gave a natural opportunity for functional binding. We looked at the COBOL, Pascal, and Fortran subsets to see how many developers seized the opportunity to encapsulate the algorithm in its own module. More than three-quarters of all the programs analyzed did encapsulate the algorithm, giving good evidence that programmers are mindful of binding strength.

Those who did hit upon the functionally bound module were nearly twice as likely to pass the acid test of correctness. Those who did not hit upon the functionally bound module were four times as likely to end up in the 4th performance quartile (based on speed and accuracy) as in the 1st.

Hypothesis 4 (data hiding): Not confirmed

The principle of data hiding as a basis for modularization is presented in [7], and more recently in [8]. There was a clear opportunity in the Coding War Games problem to encapsulate and thus conceal an awkward data structure. A modular design that takes advantage of this opportunity yielded a slightly better readability, in our opinion. Yet none of the subset of programs analyzed did encapsulate the data structure.

Our assessment on this point is weak because the awkward data structure was not *very* awkward. Had it been more unwieldy, perhaps more developers would have tried to conceal it within a module. All we have found is a lack of evidence that programmers are looking aggressively to hide complexity.

Hypothesis 5 (cleanroom methods): Weakly confirmed

The term *cleanroom development,* first coined by Harlan Mills, implies a development process that emphasizes correct initial program construction, rather than cycles of coding and repair. In its most common form, developers either code or test, but not both; those who write the code have had the last chance to save their honor (avoid defects) when they announce the product is ready for test. The Coding War Games required a total separation of code and test.

After a controlled experiment on the use of cleanroom methods, Selby, Basili, and Baker reported in [9] that 86 percent of participants had complained of missing the satisfaction of testing their own code, but 81 percent nonetheless said they would use the method again. Resultant product quality was excellent.

Our findings were similar. The most frequent comment from participants was objection to cleanroom procedures. However, more than one-third of all participants did deliver zero-defect products, even without the opportunity to test and repair. The exercise was small, but not trivial. It involved an average length of 163 Pascal statements or 234 COBOL statements. The fact that cleanroom novices could perform so well in this mode is an encouraging sign.

Hypothesis 6 (use of structured coding): Confirmed

A frequently repeated horror story among consultants is that the 1970s never happened at such-and-such corporation, where spaghetti-bowl coding is the invariant rule. Our sample gave little evidence of this (perhaps apocryphal) effect. Programs were mostly well structured and sensibly indented to call attention to control subordination.

There was more goto use than we might have expected. In the Pascal subset, for example, fully 21 percent of the programs had goto statements. We looked at each incident of goto use to understand the developers' rationale for this possible violation of structured programming technique. Of the 105 goto statements analyzed, the vast majority were emergency exits or loop exits, in keeping with the disciplined use of gotos suggested by Knuth and by Zahn [10, 11]. Fewer than 4 percent of the programs could be judged unstructured.

The COBOL subset was slightly less pure in its use of structured programming. The average program had 11 subroutine invocations and 8 gotos. Again, the gotos were mostly used to implement sensible structured programming constructs not directly supported by the language.

Hypothesis 7 (convergence of design): Refuted

An argument for a strong, centrally enforced Methodology is that any two developers would be inclined to come up with the same design for a given specification.

One company, known for its almost religiously imposed Methodology, had 16 participants in the 1987 Games. All had been trained in The Methodology. There was no sign at all of convergence of design concept among the 16. Their programs had as few as 4 and as many as 23 modules with an even distribution between the extremes. They didn't even code in a very similar style (from 0 to 17 gotos, a nearly 3-to-1 variation in total program length).

4. ANOMALIES DETECTED EN ROUTE

Looking over the code, we observed three pronounced patterns that, although they don't pertain precisely to the theme of this paper, seem worth noting.

The first is a surprising variation in program length. For those who hope to treat length as an indication of function size, the variation of nearly 10-to-1 across a sample of programs in the same language and written to the same specification is truly daunting. Figure 2, presented below, shows the variation in program length for the COBOL community.

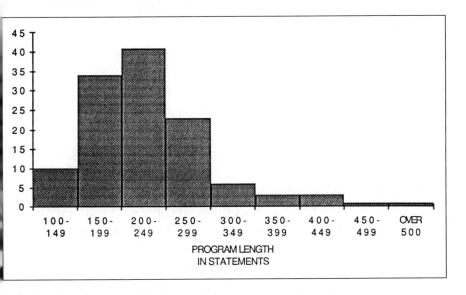

Figure 2. Distribution by program length (COBOL only).

The observed variation is bound to raise questions about our counting standard. For the record, we performed a syntax-directed count of executable and declaration statements, excluding comments and blank lines. We defined *total length* as the sum of executable statements and declaration statements. To achieve some uniformity between languages, we didn't count braces in C, nor BEGINs and ENDs in other languages. All counts were conducted to a written standard.

Since we had so many programmers who hit upon the same functionally bound module, we used that module as the basis for a detailed analysis of varying length. All the modules analyzed were functionally identical. The count of statements, however, varied for this single tiny module by a factor of eight. When we counted lines instead of statements, the variation was greater. This seemed like an ideal opportunity to experiment in the use of some of the Halstead metrics [12]. We computed Halstead's length, vocabulary, and volume for a subset of the modules. Each of the Halstead metrics succeeded to some degree in damping out the variation. Consider the maximum divided by the minimum for different ways of assessing the module's size:

Size Measurement	Max/min
Statement count	8.00
Halstead's length	1.73
Vocabulary	1.59
Volume	1.94

The second pattern observed is the variation in the number of variables used. In the Pascal community, for example, the average number of variables used was 20. But some programmers used as few as 7, and others as many as 42. Those who used more variables had proportionately longer programs.

The third pattern is that those who wrote more verbose programs took longer to do the work and had a higher defect rate than those who wrote spare programs. This would not have been thought an anomaly at all in the 1970s. But current conventional wisdom is that spare programs might be tighter and so harder to deal with. Our data indicate otherwise.

REFERENCES

[1]   M. Dyer, R.C. Linger, and H.D. Mills, "Cleanroom Software Engineering," *IEEE Software,* September 1987, pp. 19-25.

[2]   T. DeMarco and T. Lister, "Programmer Performance and the Effects of the Workplace," *Proceedings of the 8th International Conference on Software Engineering* (London: 1985), pp. 268-72.

[3]   H.D. Mills, "Top-Down Programming in Large Systems," *Debugging Techniques in Large Systems,* ed. R. Rustin (Englewood Cliffs, N.J.: Prentice-Hall, 1971).

[4]   G.J. Myers, *Reliable Software Through Composite Design* (New York: Petrocelli/Charter, 1975).

[5]   W. Stevens, G.J. Myers, and L.L. Constantine, "Structured Design," *IBM Systems Journal,* Vol. 13, No. 2 (May 1974).

[6]   E. Yourdon and L.L. Constantine, *Structured Design: Fundamentals of a Discipline of Computer Program and Systems Design,* 2nd ed. (Englewood Cliffs, N.J.: Prentice-Hall, 1979). (1979 edition of Yourdon Press's 1975 text.)

[7]   D.L. Parnas, "On the Criteria to Be Used in Decomposing Systems into Modules," *Communications of the ACM,* Vol. 15, No. 12 (December 1972), pp. 1053-58.

[8]   G. Booch, *Software Engineering with Ada* (Menlo Park, Calif.: Benjamin Cummings Publishing Co., 1983).

[9]   R.W. Selby, V.R. Basili, and F.T. Baker, "Cleanroom Software Development: An Empirical Evaluation," *IEEE Transactions on Software Engineering,* Vol. SE-13, No. 9 (September 1987), pp. 1027-37. Reprinted in *Software State-of-the-Art: Selected Papers,* eds. T. DeMarco and T. Lister (New York: Dorset House Publishing, 1990), pp. 256-76.

[10]   D.E. Knuth, "Structured Programming with Go To Statements," *Current Trends in Programming Methodology,* ed. R.T. Yeh (Englewood Cliffs, N.J.: Prentice-Hall, 1977).

[11]   C.T. Zahn, "A Control Statement for Natural Top-Down Structured Programming," *Symposium on Programming Languages* (Paris: 1974).

[12]   M.H. Halstead, *Elements of Software Science* (New York: American Elsevier, 1977).

11

SOFTWARE PRODUCTIVITY: THE COVERT AGENDA

Perhaps I was affected by too many French and Italian movies in my youth, but I swear I can often see subtitles in the air when people are speaking. Oddly, the subtitles I see almost always seem to be saying something quite different from what the speaker's actual words are. This leads me to the strange conclusion that people, even when they speak with the utmost sincerity, sometimes mean the opposite of what they say.

11

SOFTWARE PRODUCTIVITY:
THE COVERT AGENDA

Reprinted from *Deadline*, May 1988.

Imagine, if you will, one of those all-too-frequent management meetings on the subject of "the software crisis." Seated around the walnut table are the corporation's silver foxes, their immaculately coiffed white hair, $800 suits, and gold-link watch bands in silent testimony of their rise to senior management. In charge of all this splendor is the Big Cheese. Seated well down the table is sure to be one very unhappy-looking person, the manager in charge of Software Development. He or she can be forgiven for not looking forward to what is about to happen.

The B.C. calls the meeting to order. Terms of the crisis are laid out like an indictment:

- The software development process is out of control.
- Overruns are rampant on software projects.
- Busted budgets are the rule, not the exception.
- The backlog of waiting applications grows longer every day.
- Higher software productivity is needed immediately. Much higher. Maybe even much, much higher.

(This is the B.C. talking here, not your author; your author thinks this particular indictment is a lot of hogwash. But more about that later.)

Now the real fun begins. Each of the silver foxes weighs in with an opinion about what needs to be done. There are at least a dozen ponderous and pompous views from people who have never written a program in their lives. The further afield the speakers' experience lies from software, the more simplistic their solutions. All of the speakers are utterly certain of the wisdom of their statements. It must be nice to be so certain. Maybe it comes from having an $800 suit and a gold-link watchband.

One fellow from Finance quotes from a feature article on the software dilemma, published in London's prestigious *The Economist*. The feature writer asks rhetorically, "When will the software community wake up and embrace the new methods that work?" The particular new method he has in mind is something called VDM, or the Vienna Development Methodology. VDM is one of a long line of panaceas. If the article had been written a year ago, it would have been Prolog; and if it had been written the year before that, it would have been 4GLs.

"When will our software group wake up and use the new methods that work? Like this VDR, or whatever it's called." This is no rhetorical question. The silver fox is glaring in annoyance down the table at the software manager.

"Yes. Well," the manager replies, "we sent some of our people to a seminar on VDM. It involves writing down your specifications in a formal meta-language that unfortunately can't even be typed on a regular keyboard. It looks kind of like Sanskrit."

But this is all just detail. Nobody gets to be a silver fox by being interested in detail. By the time the meeting is over, all the points have been neatly written down in the minutes. They will be worked up by the B.C. into an Agenda for Software Productivity Improvement, which will eventually have as many as half-a-dozen specific points. The software manager summarizes these with just one note scrawled on a yellow pad: "Find panacea, fast."

Before the improvement agenda is published, though, it will be reworked by consultants. These consultants are people who *have* written programs. They have also designed programs and written specifications and managed projects. (But they will never do any of these things again, having found a more lucrative line of work.) By the time they have finished massaging the document, most of the more vaporous ideas have been removed. Gone is any explicit mention of VDM, since that would be too easy to shoot down. The final result usually lists points such as these:

1. Adopt a new methodology.
2. Incorporate the very latest techniques.
3. Centralize control of the software process.
4. Tighten up on extraneous costs.
5. Buy productivity tools.

Now what could be wrong with that? I must have seen twenty or more such agendas over the years, handed down from on high in client companies. They have begun to depress me, not so much for what they say as what they don't say. They are utterly oriented toward the technology of the software process, and pay not even lip service to the even more essential sociology that makes projects work.

To make matters worse, actions taken in the technological arena are bound to have side effects, usually negative, in the sociological arena. Imposing a methodology or centralizing control may give some technological gain, but that could be more than offset if the developers' sense of being in charge of their own work began to suffer. Programs to "tighten up on extraneous costs" often boil down to cutting training budgets or reducing work space, measures that are bound to be felt strongly and negatively by the developer. All of these actions are likely to translate into increased employee dissatisfaction, perhaps leading to the loss of key people.

None of this implies, of course, that we ought not to try to improve productivity. It only says that tinkering with the technology of the process cannot be the whole answer. In particular, trying to improve the technology in any centralized fashion without even monitoring the sociological disruption is a blunder.

But now consider the possibility that the written agenda may be only the visible part of a more extensive productivity-raising scheme. In most organizations, there is also a covert agenda for increased productivity. If the overt portion of the agenda is subject to unwelcome sociological side effects, the covert portion is a recipe for disaster. The covert agenda has two principal items:

1. Apply pressure to developers to get them to work longer and harder: Promote an ethic of workaholism; get project members to sacrifice their personal lives; gull them into accepting hopeless schedules; and then hold their feet to the fire to make them deliver.

2. Minimize product quality: Over-constrain projects so that they have to compromise quality; establish an unwritten standard that nothing beyond the minimum quality that can be crammed down the user's throat will be tolerated.

The covert agenda is covert because it can't be written down. It can't be spoken out loud without causing disbelief and rebellion. But it's there. You feel it in every aspect of the scheduling and budgeting process.

PROGRAMMER:	"Boss, you asked me to estimate how long this job will take. I think I can have it for you in five months."
BOSS:	"Kid, I can't let you box yourself in like that. Five months isn't nearly enough." (The boss is sure the job couldn't possibly be done in less than a year.) "I'm going to give you *seven* months."

What's at fault here is not the individual manager, but rather the idea, so widely accepted in the software world, that estimates and schedules are to serve a function as motivators. The purpose of the schedule, in this view, is not to give a business-like assessment of when the product will probably be done, but rather to put project members under tremendous pressure. The programmer quoted above, once realizing that the job is way underbudgeted, will try to make up for it by compromising his personal life (working overtime) and by compromising quality (leaving out things the user will need but forgot to demand, sliding problems under the rug to be dealt with in maintenance, or delivering a just barely stable product).

It all seems to work in the short term. Developers do put in enormous overtime, particularly if they have participated (naively) in the estimates. Not one bit of "unnecessary" quality has to be paid for. The manager can demonstrate increased productivity by the simple (fraudulent) means of dividing work accomplished by hours paid, rather than by hours worked. The problem becomes visible only in the long run. Workers begin to hate themselves for compromising their own quality standards. They know who is to blame: "I work for a company that doesn't give a damn for quality; all it cares about is shoving the product out the door by April 1." They begin to feel used, realizing all the weekends and overtime hours that have been extracted directly from their family lives. They're soon on their way to a new job.

In Tracy Kidder's book *The Soul of a New Machine,* he details the story of a project conducted at breakneck speed, under incredible pressure piled on by management [1]. All the team members become obsessed with trying to achieve the impossible. They work through nights and weekends over the course of more than a year. In a postmortem at the end, Kidder reflects that the team did accomplish some of the nearly impossible goals by the simple expedient of working in excess of a hundred hours a week each. He also mentions the fact, almost as an afterthought, that at the end of the project, the entire staff quit. Not just some of them, but every single one. Now, in light of the presence of a covert agenda, let's go back and examine the indictment of software developers:

- Is the software development process out of control? If it is, it's only because meaningful estimates and controls have been given up in order to use the entire scheduling process as a means of applying pressure.

- Are overruns and busted budgets happening too frequently? When performance doesn't meet the estimate, there are two possible causes: poor performance or poor estimates. In the software world, we have ample evidence that our estimates stink, but virtually no evidence that people in general don't work hard enough or intelligently enough.

- Is the backlog growing longer and longer? A project that will actually cost $2 million when complete, may be started with an expected cost of $1 million. While it was still on the backlog, its expected cost was bandied about at an even lower figure. The expected benefits are often far less than the actual cost can ever be. Such projects shouldn't have been on the backlog at all, but on the reject pile.

- Is much higher productivity needed *immediately?* Sure, just like we need an immediate cure for cancer and for AIDS. It's not on the horizon, though. A real improvement of 12 percent or 15 percent may be possible with a carefully thought-out program. Improvements of 100 percent or more are pure hype.

The covert agenda hurts us where we are already hurting. It causes demotivation, burnout, and increased loss of our best workers. It's an insidious cost, because it's only visible in the long run.

Lots of companies have risen above the transient attractions of the covert agenda. You know who they are, the companies that don't have a turnover problem, where people are so loyal and turned on that they wouldn't leave for anything. They defeat the covert agenda by the simple and mature decision not to allow it to be covert. When reformulated and stated in black and white, the old covert agenda items take on a brand-new light. They focus on two important questions:

1. *How much pressure (as indicated by overtime) is in our best interest over the long term?*

   The most successful companies allow a little pressure from time to time, but realize that a lot of pressure and a lot of overtime are signs of managerial bankruptcy.

2. *How much quality shall we put into our products?*

   Simply asking this question leads you naturally into the business of defining and collecting quality metrics. If you're also collecting productivity metrics, you'll soon learn that the two are linked. Allowing developers to strive for quality even far beyond the needs of the user is sure to boost productivity more than enough to break even.

REFERENCE

[1]   T. Kidder, *The Soul of a New Machine* (Boston: Atlantic-Little, Brown Books, 1981).

12

TAKING A SECOND LOOK
AT THE SOFTWARE FACTORY

The following piece was prepared as a teaser for a presentation I made to the Fifth Annual Monterey Software Conference in April 1993. While the tease may seem considered and thoughtfully sober (like all my writing), my real feelings on this subject are more extreme. I think factory methods for software are dead wrong, witless, and counter-effective. Organizations that build good software know that software is an R&D activity, not a production activity. Organizations that try to make it into a production activity produce bad software (though potentially lots of it), and they miss the opportunity to be part of the transformation that software has effected on the rest of the world since the 1970s.

12

TAKING A SECOND LOOK
AT THE SOFTWARE FACTORY

Not previously published.

Everyone wants to build a software factory, but no one wants to work in one. The reason for this is that building one looks to be an amusing task, but working in one looks deadly. Before we go charging ahead into the age of the software factory, let's pause a moment to consider whether we ought to be charging in exactly the opposite direction.

In this short philosophical statement, I propose to lay down a basis for thinking about software factories in general, and about the pros and cons of transforming your own organization into one in particular.

THE CASE FOR THE SOFTWARE FACTORY

The case for the software factory is set out persuasively in Michael Cusumano's recent book, *Japan's Software Factories: A Challenge to U.S. Management,* and in a related article in *The Wall Street Journal* [1, 2]. The argument there is that just as we software folk are forever automating other people's business, we ought to get on with automating our own. The Japanese, as Cusumano tells us, have applied true factory methods to software development, complete with uniform dress, uniform methods, and uniform workplace:

> *The details vary, but the basic concept of the "software factory"*
> *is the same. American companies tend to treat software as an art;*

149

the Japanese have tried to make the process something done by rote. . . . Hitachi is considered the pioneer, building its first software factory in 1969 and opening its 7,000-employee plant here two years ago. It seems as much like a factory as a white-collar office can. The programs are written in 60 different work units, identically laid out in even rows, down to the placement of the computers on each desk. . . . Japanese employees keep detailed records of every keystroke.

The result of all this, according to Cusumano, is a rate of productivity that puts American industry to shame, coupled with better quality. Specifically, he writes, "Japanese companies averaged 50 percent to 70 percent higher output per programmer, and one-third to one-half the level of errors."

YES, BUT . . .

When you examine the productivity figures in the literature about software factories, they are invariably expressed in lines of code per programmer-day. When you multiply the productivity times the huge number of people who are supposed to be that productive, you get the most amazing result of all: a total code production rate that boggles the mind. For example, one factory set up by a Japanese General Electric subsidiary and documented as part of the literature on software factories had a computed production rate of more than 500 million lines of code per year. Now I have a grumpy question for you: What the hell do they do with all that code? That one factory, set up in 1984, should by now have produced nearly five billion lines of code (assuming no productivity improvement since 1984; otherwise, it's even more). That's more code than was generated by Microsoft, Apple, and IBM during the same period.

There is only one thing you can do with that much code: Retire it quickly. And that is not part of the solution, but part of the problem. In fact, generating enormous quantities of code has never been a primary goal of the software industry. When we're good, it's not because of the billions and billions of lines of code we produce; and when we're not so good, it's not because we didn't produce enough.

Quite the opposite is true. A company like Intuit can produce the popular accounting program Quicken® and stand the entire software industry on its ear. What's so great about Quicken? Its enormous size? No, the thing is dinky. What's great about Quicken is that it is useful, clean, learnable, and specifically targeted to fill the needs perfectly of a very real market segment. The company spent all its energy and capital on learning the needs of that market and meeting them with style and elegance. Intuit's people produced a small program, but an extremely good one. Then they went right back into design mode and made it better and better with every release.

A recent article in *The Economist* compares the successes and failures of the software industry with those in the aircraft industry [3]:

> Broadly, there are three sorts of failure in big engineering projects: the Concorde, the Comet and the Spruce Goose. Concorde-type failures . . . simply cost too much and take too long to be worthwhile. Comet-type failures are . . . unplanned and unfortunate experiments.

You may remember the Comet: It was the plane that kept falling out of the sky due to metal fatigue. Sure, we do have some projects like that. They are failures, but honorable failures. We get blind-sided by risks we hadn't anticipated and another project goes belly up. There are some Concorde-type projects, too, that come to naught. Again, they are honorable failures, undone by their overlarge ambition and imperfect risk assessment. But Spruce Goose-type failures are different. From the same article:

> It was widely thought that Howard Hughes's folie de grandeur— a vast sea-plane made of wood—would not fly, and except for one lumbering climb to the heady altitude of 70 feet, it did not. But once he had embarked upon it, Hughes felt he could not stop without losing face. Spruce Goose projects are badly conceived, badly executed and often pointless.

Pointless is the key word here. Maybe my own consulting exposes me to a disproportionate number of Spruce Goose projects, but I am becoming convinced that they are the major problem of our industry.

Software factories, of course, do everything to make projects go faster and nothing to help them go in the right direction. As such, they don't respond to the real problems of our work. They do harm rather than good, because by putting the workers on automatic pilot, they disarm the most important correction mechanism we have.

AUTOMATING OURSELVES

Now let's go back to that idea of automating ourselves the way we have always automated others. Yes, we should do that, we should do exactly that.

That doesn't mean turning people into robots. When we automate a payroll department, for example, we don't define a set of deterministic procedures and force payroll clerks to do them by rote. No, we free people from doing rote work, by sticking that work inside computers. The people are left to do those things that cannot be done by rote.

So, too, in software. We automate what we can and put the rest into the hands of knowledge workers. The tasks of those knowledge workers become less factory-like with each such improvement.

When we have automated all those elements of software production that are or can be made deterministic, the software developer will be left with work that is more conceptual than ever. He or she will be nothing like a factory worker. We will then have transformed ourselves into something that makes a lot more sense than a software factory: a software unfactory.

REFERENCES

[1]   M. Cusumano, *Japan's Software Factories: A Challenge to U.S. Management* (New York: Oxford University Press, 1991).
[2]   *The Wall Street Journal,* Feb. 8, 1991.
[3]   *The Economist,* March 10, 1993.

13

THE CHOIR AND THE TEAM

This essay was the result of an experiment conducted during one of the annual meetings of The Atlantic Systems Guild. We assembled ourselves that year in princely digs at Hampton Court outside London (you can rent charming little homes right on the castle grounds). The experiment was to put our heads together and sing. . . .

13

THE CHOIR AND THE TEAM

Not previously published.

Corporate political correctness of our day requires that we all be staunch supporters of teams and teamwork. Even the occasional manager who is secretly threatened by tightly knit teams is obliged to mouth formulaic statements to the effect that "we're all team players here," sometimes even while working quietly to undermine the whole notion. (Such a manager is particularly likely to display one of those odious framed plaques celebrating teamwork on his or her office wall.) There is just no place in the modern corporation for people who don't talk a good line about teams.

But talk is cheap. For all the talk, teams don't work very well in most of the organizations I visit. They jell rarely and sometimes they don't stay jelled. Most of the groups that are called teams aren't.

Now I, of course, am a staunch supporter of teams and teamwork. I really am. Honest. So please read what follows with that thought in mind. If you don't, you may think I'm suggesting that we ought to throw the whole concept of teams out the window. . . .

We ought to throw the whole concept of teams out the window. There is something so wrongheaded about what we're trying to accomplish in forming teams that its success could be our undoing. We're trying to pattern our work groups on athletic teams. The metaphor of athletic endeavor is simply incompatible with what the work groups in a happy organization are all about.

Here, I am not referring alone to the fact that prototypical teams, the professional sports teams that we read about endlessly, are often populated by selfish, overcompensated egomaniacs. It's more than that. Intrinsic to athletic teamwork is a kind of competition that is directly at odds with successful corporate practice.

Before I develop this theme, I offer the following as a preview: In my personal inter-ear database of management experience, there is a nearly perfect correlation between dreadful management and a propensity to use Vince Lombardi quotes.

Athletic teams are meant to compete. They compete with other teams, the enemy. But members of each team also compete with each other. There is a pecking order within the team and competition to rise within it. One's level in the order is determined by playing time, position, and salary (more obscene salaries have pecking privileges on the less obscene). The business of overtaking teammates is as important as, if not more important than, besting the other teams. It is this element of internal competition that is particularly out of place in work groups.

Internal competition results in the sense that one player can win, even though the team is losing. He or she wins by moving up in the pecking order. Some of the factors that lead to the team's overall loss may even benefit the individual who is moving ahead. So the starting quarterback's terrible day is a direct contributor to the team's defeat, but a bit of incredible good luck for the second-string quarterback who got the chance to throw that one great pass.

When we use the athletic-teams formula in shaping a work group, we inherit some of the bad features along with the good. The most injurious of the bad is a tendency toward competition among group members. But wait, isn't competition good? Isn't competition part of the all-American way? Doesn't it act to clean out the deadwood, to keep everyone focused? Yes and no. We can certainly keep the adrenaline high by fostering competition. Imagine, for example, an organization in which everyone gets shot except the highest performer. What is lost in this model is the possibility of effective cooperation. Since the kind of work we typically do depends more for its success on cooperation than on extremes of performance in one or two individuals, competition works against us.

Whenever I see teams that aren't pulling together, there is always internal competition at work. Individuals are not signing on to the common goal because they have better options for individual advancement if they don't.

Some managers will even tell you that a little competition in the team is a good thing. "Keeps them on their toes," they'll say. They remind me of the rather sad parent who thinks it's okay that his kids compete with each other. What's sad is that the competition always comes first, and the thought that it's okay comes later, not as an opinion but a rationalization. Competition isn't okay. When siblings compete with each other, it's often because there isn't enough parental affection and respect to keep them all nourished. Children who grow up in such families can be scarred by the experience. They have trouble cooperating and forming warm, trusting relationships and, as adults, often remain distanced from their siblings. Similarly, competition within a team can be a result of ungiving management, of too little respect to be shared.

The problem with the athletic metaphor is that it makes such management acceptable, and it makes the individual's choice to ignore common goals seem reasonable and admirable.

What I'd like to throw out the window is not the entire social structure of what we now call a "team," but just the team metaphor. In its place we need another, one that calls attention to harmony and cooperation. It should stress that individual success cannot be separated from success of the group: You can't succeed while the group is failing, nor can you fail when it succeeds. There are many candidate metaphors that effectively tie these two levels of success together. The most appealing, to my mind, is that of the choir.

Of course, in a choir, the individual can only succeed to the extent that the whole prospers. (No one will ever tell you that the group was horribly sour but you sounded fine.) And the whole can only prosper to the extent that everyone does well. This is a particularly apt metaphor for software work because the perceived quality of a software product is equivalent to the quality of its weakest link. If some people's modules are of low quality, even the most heroic quality achievement of other individuals will be invisible. In this environment, cooperation matters a lot more than individual heroics.

A problem with the musical metaphor is that so many of us pass through the schools without learning anything about music. I, for example, was a solid A student all through school, but an illiterate in music, a triumph of our educational system. Even the image that I tried out in the preceding paragraph—you, being part of a choir—may feel strange if you have never had the pleasure of singing harmony.

I myself had never had that pleasure until very recently. The part of the brain where some people have musical ability was in mine just a vast emptiness. I was feeling that some minimal experience with musical harmony might help me better understand the harmonious work that is so apparent in effective work groups. With this in mind, I enlisted the other members of our Guild, always good-natured experimenters, and we hired a singing teacher. She taught us to open our throats, lean our heads together, and sing. The object of the exercise was not what each of us learned, but the joint experience of those first few sweet harmonies we produced. They arrived in an oddly moving moment. There was a silence as the notes died out, some embarrassed laughter, and tears in the corners of a few eyes.

What's the point? Are we better co-workers for the music we learned to make? I can't say that; I certainly couldn't prove it to you, either. I wouldn't dare to suggest that your people would make better software together if they took some music lessons first. (But I wouldn't rule it out either.) What I can say is that we came away with a better metaphor for our joint interaction: the harmonious work group.

I am never going to feel again as positively about the word *team* as I used to. It's not what I'm trying to build any longer. When I do my best now to help a group of individuals become a unified force, I know the object has to be not teamwork, but harmony.

14

Icons

I wrote this essay after reading Don Norman's extraordinary book, *The Design of Everyday Things* [1]. If you've read his work, you know that Norman makes a cult of elegant design, whereby "elegant" is defined entirely in terms of the ease and pleasure of use of something. The more I followed his thesis, the more I came to believe that the Macintosh on my desk is one of the best examples of such elegance. It has become for me a symbol of the kind of software design I have been trying to achieve, and trying to help my clients achieve.

14

Icons

I bought my first Macintosh in early 1985. Since that time, I have gone through stages well known to most Macintosh users: from Amused to Intrigued to Persuaded and finally into the nether reaches of Bigotry. I work at my Mac most days. The work consists of some writing, some modeling, and some desktop video. I also maintain my company's accounts on the Mac. In the course of a week, I use a hundred or more different programs. When I'm on the road, I carry a PowerBook®.

That's me. Now let me tell you something about you; not you, the actual person who is reading this page, but you, the statistically abstracted average reader, my audience: You are five-foot-seven. You have approximately 1.0 breasts (statistics is funny about these things). You're a trifle overweight, and—most important for my purposes in this article—you *don't* use a Mac. What you use is an IBM 286- or 386-based PC® or a clone thereof. Poor you.

This is going to be one of those articles that tries to show you how inadequate your principal work tool is. It will say outrageous things like "The average blue-collar worker in the U.S. has $35,000 of capital equipment supporting his or her job. So, how come your company is too cheap to buy you a real computer?" And so on. You may have come across such articles before. This is not the first.

Before I get on with my diatribe, it's worth digressing a bit to mention just what is the purpose of an article like this. It is not to persuade you to change computers. That would be silly.

You're not going to change. You're probably locked to your computer and its operating system by corporate decision, by habit, or by the grim realization that you have invested most of your youth learning why and when to press control-alt-# and other unlikely key combinations. No, you're not going to switch. In fact, getting you to switch plays no part in my intentions. The purpose of this article (and of others like it) is *to demonstrate the moral superiority of the author.*

I say that, of course, in jest. Yet there is a germ of truth in the idea that an extraordinarily elegant design confers a certain nobility on those who work with it and recognize it as such. The Mac interface is an extraordinarily elegant design. It is practically an icon of good design. I think of myself, as you probably think of yourself, as a software designer. Icons are important to us. Good design is important to us. The Mac is a symbol of what we are trying to stand for.

The Mac on my desk sets a standard that I respect. It is a symbol of doing something right in the first place, rather than doing it quick and dirty and then patching it up forever after. If the Mac interface is an icon of good design, then DOS and OS/2® and even Windows™ are icons of bad design. Trying to create a good design with a DOS machine on your desk is like trying to cook a great meal in a sewer. It's not what the machine does for you or doesn't do for you that matters here; it's how it makes you feel.

None of this applies to users who are not and never have been software designers. They can make use of the most god-awful, undesigned interface by leaning on the shift and control keys with one elbow while keying in a chord of meaningless characters to get something done. They may find it distasteful to have to remember so many arbitrary conventions, but, hey, they think, that's computers for you.

You and I are different. It hurts us to make such compromises. It hurts to do something that doesn't make sense or to use a procedure that won't stick in the mind. When we've made these compromises enough times, they may not hurt anymore, but that's even worse. It means that something inside us has gone dead, something that recognized and railed against bad design.

A little bit of our design sense has been numbed and we are diminished.

A good software design is distinguished from a bad or mediocre one by two characteristics:

1. The product fits easily into the user's mind and habits.
2. Its internal structure is easy to understand, adapt, and enhance.

By both of these measures, the Mac is a masterpiece of design, and DOS and its derivatives come up lacking.

You could make the case that DOS and OS/2 were not designed at all; they were just coded and debugged (or, in the case of OS/2, coded and partially debugged). What is missing from both is any evidence of extended clear thinking at the conceptual and architectural levels. OS/2 is a rehash of DOS, which was a rehash of CPM®, which was a hodgepodge of features from older DEC minicomputer operating systems. The great leap forward that illuminates the Mac desktop (and the NeXT® desktop as well and, to some degree, the Open Look® desktop) seems not to have been noticed in the IBM PC and PS/2® world. So we have command line architectures still, in an era when the rest of the world has moved on. And, because so much of OS/2 and DOS has been carried over unexamined from CPM, they are not even good command line architectures. (Unix® was a good command line architecture.)

People on the Mac project, on the other hand, spent most of their energies in design. They designed a concept (the desktop), a set of tools (the programmer's workbench), an operating system (the finder), and a sociology (the closely supported developer community) to carry a uniform philosophy to the application level. The result is that the hundred or so programs I use every week have a common organic order that assures I never have to use a manual or remember anything arbitrary. The learning curve on the Mac is short, and the learning curve on most Mac applications is zero.

We have just seen a major new deliverable from Apple, the Macintosh System 7. The entire look of the desktop has been changed. The use of colors and hues is astonishing. The system incorporates support for moving graphics (Quicktime®), 24-bit color, elegant networking, amazing sounds, video interfaces, remote desktop, an entirely reworked finder, and a host of other wonders. In spite of all the changes, the integrity of the idiom has been preserved. Nothing you learned under the prior systems has to be relearned.

What's surprising about System 7 is that the project could be done at all. It is a tribute to the design concept of the Macintosh that a few hundred people, formed into a highly motivated team, could do so much enhancement in just a little over two years.

If OS/2 is ever delivered, I predict it will become as immutable as DOS: There will never be an enhancement to OS/2 as ambitious as System 7. Because all the effort has been in coding, debugging, and support, not in design, the system will be unchangeable. It may be even worse than unchangeable; it may be *unfinishable*. IBM reports that it is now spending $350 million a year to wrap up OS/2 [2]. That works out to nearly 5,000 people. Such is the cost of implementing first and designing later.

So far, I haven't said much about Windows. Is it relevant? Is it usable? Yes and yes. But is it good design? No, it's a kludge. It's another attempt to patch up something that was done wrong in the first place. It's a Dusenberg body on top of a Nash engine and frame. Signs of patching are everywhere in the endless accommodations you have to make to the DOS that lives underneath. Sure, you can get work done on it, just as you could get work done with DOS or CPM. But it's still a symbol of bad software engineering. It stands for doing something wrong in the first place and then fixing and fixing and fixing.

The Mac is an icon of good software design. It inspires me to be the best software engineer I can be. For this reason alone, it is a delight to have and to look at. I can have these pleasures without ever even turning it on.

REFERENCES

[1]   D.A. Norman, *The Design of Everyday Things* (New York: Basic Books, 1988).
[2]   *The Wall Street Journal*, Dec. 6, 1991.

15

ON NAMING A COMPANY

When we formed The Atlantic Systems Guild in 1983, the first name we chose was rejected by the State of New York. We had wanted to call ourselves just "The Systems Guild." That put us into a quandary. The only decision-making mechanism we ever figured out was unanimous consent, and it looked like we'd never be able to settle on another name. That prompted the following piece, originally distributed to Guild members only.

15

ON NAMING A COMPANY

Not previously published.

I don't pretend to have *the* name ready to propose for the guild, but after staring at the ceiling for a while and after talking with some of you, I think I have some insight to offer on the subject. I hope these notes will help you percolate better, by observing just what characteristics we're hoping that new guild name will offer us.

THE DEMARCO PATENTED NAMING METHODOLOGY

One thing that has proved helpful to me was writing down all company and association names that have been great naming successes, plus those names that have come to stand for the kind of image we're hoping to build. I thought that each successful name might suggest some sort of parallel that we could exploit. Here is my list of all-time best names and best idea-group names:

- ✓ The Bauhaus
- ✓ The Oxford Union
- ✓ The Manhattan Project
- ✓ The Rippon Society
- ✓ The Hudson Institute
- ✓ The Network for Learning
- ✓ The Systems Guild

The rest of my methodology involves trying to abstract just why good names are good and, finally, building on the pattern suggested by each of the prototype names to come up with some likely possibilities.

WHAT MAKES A GOOD NAME GOOD

All the names listed above appeal to me and, in trying to understand why, I came up with these observations:

1. The names have a certain *heroic* quality. Each one is a name that can carry on a good image, if its creators manage to develop one. Cute names (International Turtle, The Artful Smarts Company, etc.) can never be heroic, so in the long run they aren't very ambitious.
2. The names are *not self-serving* in any way. (They don't say the organizations are good, smart, structured, or anything.)
3. The names are *initially neutral.* Whatever image comes to be associated with such names is not a function of the name itself, but of what the people in the organization accomplish. Notice that except for the last two in the list, the names don't even hint at the basic subject matter that the group deals in.
4. The names are short and easy to remember and pronounce.

As four of my prototype names are geographic in nature, I started to think about what our geographic qualities are. I came up with these: Manhattan, New York, Big Apple, Hudson, Chelsea (our geographic center, and the place where our offices could very well end up).

CANDIDATE NAMES BY EXTRAPOLATION

I stared at the list of prototypes and tried to think of the best candidate guild name suggested by each one. Here is my result:

PROTOTYPE	SUGGESTED GUILD NAME
The Bauhaus	The Systems Bauhaus
The Oxford Union	The Chelsea Union
The Manhattan Project	The Hudson Project
The Rippon Society	?
The Hudson Institute	?
The Network for Learning	The Development Network
The Systems Guild	The Manhattan Systems Guild

We would have to add "Inc." or "Ltd." behind any of the names. From my list, I'm rather taken with two: The Chelsea Union, Inc., and The Hudson Project, Inc. No guarantee, of course, that any of these names are available. . . .

AFTERWORD

We eventually chose the Atlantic as our geographic element since some Guild members operate out of a London base with the others in the U.S. And so we became The Atlantic Systems Guild. We have never regretted it.

In the years since, I have continued to pay attention to good company names. My favorite today is Victoria's Secret (though it's slightly humorous and thus violates my first law to some extent). That company is not just well-named, but imaginatively managed. It was recently used by Lester Thurow of the Sloan School as an example of how multinational merchandising companies ought to be run.

Names matter a lot. We spent weeks and weeks on ours. In the rush to get a new company going, founders are often sheepish about investing this kind of effort on a mere symbol. When it's your turn to give an identity to the new company that you have created, I hope you take the time to come up with a great name.

16

Use of Video for Program Documentation

The royal high-muck-a-mucks of the 12th International Conference on Software Engineering decided that there would be two categories of paper presented there. The first class (the real papers) were given full conference honors and thirty minutes each for presentation. The second class of papers were labeled Experience Reports, and relegated to a fifteen-minute presentation each.

In all fairness, the paper that Curt Geertgens and I had written was indeed an experience report: It reported on experience with the use of video for program documentation at Aldus Corp. (since acquired by Adobe Systems). So we didn't feel bad about our categorization, even though we were supposed to. We contented ourselves by concluding that papers in the other class were probably non-experience reports. As I remember that conference, most of them were.

16

USE OF VIDEO FOR
PROGRAM DOCUMENTATION

with Curt Geertgens, Aldus Corp.

Copyright © 1990 IEEE. Reprinted, with permission, from the *Proceedings of the 12th International Conference on Software Engineering,* Nice, France, 1990.

There are two familiar variants of the documentation problem: a) you write all the internal documentation that you know you need and you pay a terrible price for it, or b) you don't write all the internal documentation that you know you need and you pay a terrible price for that.

The first variant occurs in companies that have a strong commitment to the conventional wisdom of software construction. They respect, as an article of faith, the cutesy maxim: "The job is not over until the paperwork is done." But the cost of paper documentation of program products can be daunting. Consider the following:

☐ Commercial software projects produce from 28 to 66 pages of documentation for every 1,000 lines of code [1].

☐ Projects in the DoD sector (governed by such standards as Mil-Spec 2167a) produce as much as 200 English words per line of code [2].

☐ The cost of document-generating activities is approximately 50 percent greater than the cost of all code-generating activities for a typical project [3].

The costs of not documenting program internals are less well quantified, but most development managers believe that missing and inadequate internal documentation are major contributors to the staggering cost of software maintenance.

A CASE IN POINT

Aldus Corp. was begun in 1984 by five founders/developers. As in many such ventures, the products were initially constructed in a resource- and time-constrained environment, which allowed little opportunity for documentation of program internals. The cost of inadequate documentation became increasingly apparent as successive versions of the initial product were developed. The company also added several new products and increased its engineering staff to more than sixty software builders, making the need for quality internal documentation even greater.

Paradoxically, the problem was made worse by the company's success in its market and a bounding stock price. The principal product designers (some of whom were also corporate principals) found themselves with substantial stock holdings and associated capital gains. One effect of this sudden new wealth was impatience with the idea of sitting down to hundreds of hours of drudgery to document the code. By late 1987, it seemed that the documentation was never going to be written. Some of the principals had left and the others were needed on critical new projects.

This was also a period of pronounced growth for the company. Staff was increased, more than doubling in each of several successive years. Even though the company was hiring experienced software engineers, there was still the need to bring each new hire up to speed on product internals. The learning curve was steep and expensive: *The average new hire required from four to six months to become acclimated with his or her assigned product subsystem.* The relative absence of documentation made the problem decidedly worse. Pressure to perform wasn't much of a substitute.

AN EXPERIMENT

In early 1988, Aldus Engineering's Product Adaptation group embarked on an experiment in documenting program internals on video. The perception was that this medium had a lower drudgery factor for those who had to produce the documentation, and a lower total cost. Proof of the first of these points was the enthusiasm the idea provoked among those who were asked to participate. No professional video personnel were involved: The effort was an amateur one from first to last. Project members took on roles as producer, director/stage manager, cameraman, and on-camera subject expert. One of the founders (Dave Walter) was enticed to come back and star in the first few videos.

The initial videos were planned as five afternoon filming sessions, covering data structures, display issues, screen dynamics, event handling, and portability concerns of the company's Page-Maker® product. The first session was at the end of January 1988.

The following logistics were proposed for the first videos (and found to be workable for the rest):

1. Each video shot in 10- to 45-minute takes, one take per topic.
2. Presentation in front of a small (10- to 12-person) live audience.
3. Audience made up of other experts to ensure accuracy, complete coverage, and good questions.
4. Minimal interaction from the audience during each take.
5. Q&A period (off-camera) after each take.
6. On-camera recap of Q&A.
7. Guest speakers brought on-camera by the principal speaker to present some subtopics.
8. Simple OHP (overhead projector) technology and whiteboards used for graphics and listed points.
9. Moderator to introduce topics and speaker, and to set the stage.

The intention was to produce serviceable rough videos, rather than polished products. For this reason, there were no retakes; when speakers flubbed or misspoke, they simply corrected themselves and went on.

ASSESSING THE RESULTS

In an informal assessment, viewers of the videos provided positive feedback. They pointed out that the videos had become essential to the training of new product personnel, since they contained much information that wasn't recorded elsewhere. An additional benefit was that the videos gave some insight about the personality and thought processes of one of the principal designers.

The cost was minimal: Initial equipment cost was less than $2,500. (The equipment had been acquired for other uses within the company, so the project actually incurred no equipment cost.) The total effort spent producing the videos, aside from the speakers' preparation, was on the order of two to three times their running time. There seems to have been no real drudgery involved in either producing or viewing the videos.

Viewers reported that they considered the experience worthwhile and essential to their subsequent understanding of the subjects discussed. The following quote is taken from a response to the survey questionnaire distributed to video users:

> The designer's intent was clearer in the videos than in any written design documentation I've ever seen. Being able to hear in the designer's own words his point-of-view, focus, approaches evaluated and rejected, etc., provides a framework in which new design decisions can be made.

To date, approximately half of the company's developers have viewed the videos. Many users reported that they viewed all or some of the tapes more than once.

FUTURE PLANS

The company's success in documenting program internals on video has been sufficient to encourage three new uses of the medium:

☐ Project Postmortems: When the project is complete, the inclination to sit down and write text drops from its normal value (low) to near zero. Yet postmortem roundtable dis-cussions can be lively and informative. Video is an ideal medium to capture the result.

☐ More "Meet the Experts" Videos: It often happens that indi-viduals become resident experts in key technology areas. Demand for their services assures that they rarely have time to sit down and produce documentation of what they know best. Transferring one's knowledge of new technology to others, a significant problem in any organization, becomes a real challenge in a small, fast-paced high-tech company. As an initial effort, we plan a series of video lectures on digital halftoning, color, dithering, resolution matching, compression, color separation, composition, and printing for desktop publishing, each topic to be presented by the company's in-house expert.

☐ Description of the Development Process: Video seems likely to be better received than the typical "fat book" presentation. It affords the opportunity to present a sometimes dry subject like software standards with enthusiasm and even passion.

SUMMARY AND CONCLUSIONS

The observation that so much of the software development dollar goes into producing narrative text might lead you to consider two different solutions:

1) Get better tools and build better skills for generating textual documentation, or
2) Learn to live with less text.

Our experience is that the second of these is feasible and prom-ising when video is used as a substitute for text. We believe that many other areas of software engineering could also benefit from the application of video technology to the documentation pro-cess. The attractively low cost of video documentation stems from the relative ease of getting people to talk instead of write and to view instead of read. It may prove that "video-assisted" software engineering is indeed a practical solution to the software documentation problem.

REFERENCES

[1] B.W. Boehm and P.N. Papaccio, "Understanding and Controlling Software Costs," *IEEE Transactions on Software Engineering*, Vol. 4, No. 10 (October 1988), pp. 1462-77. Reprinted in *Software State-of-the-Art: Selected Papers*, eds. T. DeMarco and T. Lister (New York: Dorset House Publishing, 1990), pp. 31-60.

[2] C. Jones, *Programming Productivity* (New York: McGraw-Hill, 1986).

[3] _____ , private correspondence, 1989.

17

STRUCTURED ANALYSIS:
THE BEGINNINGS OF A NEW DISCIPLINE

This was adapted from a Foreword I wrote to a book by Lis Delskov and Therese Lange, published in Danish as *Struktureret Analyse* in 1990. Since I couldn't read their Danish text, I had no comment to offer about it. Instead, I made of my Foreword a short history of the events of the late 1970s that led to the development of one of the structured disciplines.

17

STRUCTURED ANALYSIS: THE BEGINNINGS OF A NEW DISCIPLINE

Reprinted from *Deadline*, December 1989.

In looking back at a phenomenon that has had great impact on our industry and its work practices, one is tempted to try to take all the credit for it. Let me begin by saying that I did not invent any of the notions that today constitute structured analysis. My role was, at best, one of a packager and a popularizer. But I was there as the ideas were coming together.

For me, the first sense that there could be some structuring of the analysis process came with an introduction to the work that was being done by Doug Ross and John Brackett at SofTech, Inc., during the middle 1970s [1]. They called their invention SADT® for structured analysis design technique. The heart of SADT was a set of leveled data flow diagrams, very much like those I described in my 1978 book, *Structured Analysis and System Specification* [2]. The SADT convention called for balancing of data flows in and out and a notion of data conservation essentially identical to the conventions I was later to advocate. Since I was using SADT for years prior to my own publications on the subject, there is no way to avoid crediting Ross and Brackett for the main innovation. I convinced myself at the time that SADT was not so different from the Petri nets I had been experimenting with earlier [3]. But from my present perspective, it is clear to me that SADT was a major breakthrough; I could have played around with Petri nets for another decade and never stumbled upon the insight that Ross and Brackett provided.

I first met Ed Yourdon in 1969 or 1970, when we worked together at a small New York consulting firm called Mandate Systems, Inc., since deceased. This charming (though commercially hopeless) company was founded by one of our industry's most colorful characters, Jerry Wiener. Jerry had been responsible for part of the GE-Dartmouth time-sharing system, one of the most significant developments of the 1960s. We thought of him as the father of time-sharing, though he insisted he had only been its midwife.

During our years at Mandate Systems, Ed Yourdon and I never did get to work on the same project. I doubt that I had any effect on him whatsoever during that time, but I was aware of ground-breaking work he was doing in the area of design (in addition to putting in sixty hours a week on the exec of Com-Share's time-sharing system). My introduction to the concept of hierarchical modular design, something that had a powerful effect on my own design practice, was by way of some course material and the outline of a manuscript that he was to write with Larry Constantine [4].

After going our separate ways for most of the next seven years, Ed and I renewed our acquaintance in 1977. By this time, he was as fascinated by the idea of a structured approach to analysis as I was, and he had made some independent progress, to my mind taking a long step beyond SADT. The step may sound trivial when I relate it to you, but I am convinced that it was the cause of the discipline's subsequent success. Ed had introduced a new notation that was *much* less disarming than that of SADT. His style of data flow diagram (DFD) was something that could be shown to a user without first teaching that user a set of conventions. The Yourdon DFD just looked like a sketch of a system, the kind of sketch that the user might have made himself. It didn't need to be explained, since there was no apparent arbitrariness in it. In retrospect, it was its obvious arbitrariness that turned so many users off on SADT.

In addition, Ed had added a fourth notational element not present in SADT: the file or data store. You can prove to yourself that SADT's three-element notation—flow, process, and terminator—is sufficient to describe any system. A data store is just a special case of a process, one that has memory. There is an essential equivalence between data and process. That makes good theory, but bad practice. Introducing the data store into the DFD notation made the result considerably more palatable to nontechnical users.

In addition to supplying some good ideas himself, Ed played an important catalytic role in the late 1970s. He brought together many of the bright minds that were to shape the new discipline, including Ray Eisenstark, Chris Gane, Tim Lister, Steve McMenamin, John Palmer, Suzanne and James Robertson, Trish Sarson, and Victor Weinberg. I was privileged to be part of this exciting group. Each of its members made some contribution to the concept that eventually emerged.

My own contributions were two fairly tiny ones. One of them turned out to be important and the other, I must finally admit, totally counterproductive. The counterproductive one first: It was my idea that the analysis process could be represented as four separate modeling steps to produce current physical, current logical, new logical, and new physical models. I think time has proved that this basically correct observation has wasted more time than it saved. The problem was not the idea of the four models, but their relative weighting. I treated them all as equal, at least in my description of them. But then my examples were so heavily weighted with current physical models that people concluded analysis ought to be (at least in DeMarco's concept) largely a current physical modeling activity. Our industry then went on to sink untold man-millennia into unnecessary old-system physical modeling. This is a phenomenon that Steve McMenamin later dubbed the "current physical tarpit." I must apologize to all those people who slogged away so long in the tarpit. If I had it all to do over again, I would explain that there are four models to consider and they are, respectively:

the current physical model

the current logical model

the new logical model, and
the new physical model.

My good idea was the notion of the structured specification as the final product of analysis. It seems incredible to me now, but most of the early use of SA techniques had been only as investigatory tools. The people who were using them most effectively were content to abandon the tools once they had helped them discover the real requirement, and write a conventional textual specification.

The success of structured analysis has been far greater than I ever anticipated. I might have thought in the 1970s that at most a few hundred people would ever find the ideas useful. It never occurred to me until considerably later that SA would appeal to the commercial world; I thought of it as a technique exclusively focused on real-time system development. It has gone considerably beyond that to the extent that most analysts today either use the idea explicitly or at least find themselves affected by it. I wish I could take the credit for that, but I can't. What I do take credit for is having the good sense and good luck to be there when so many bright and creative people were doing the real work.

REFERENCES

[1]   D.T. Ross and J.W. Brackett, "An Approach to Structured Analysis: An Analysis Technique Similar to Structured Programming Enables Systems to Be Designed More Effectively," *Computer Decisions,* Vol. 7, No. 9 (September 1976), pp. 40-44.

[2]   T. DeMarco, *Structured Analysis and System Specification* (Englewood Cliffs, N.J.: Prentice-Hall, 1978).

[3]   C.A. Petri, "Kommunikation mit Automaten," Ph.D. Thesis, University of Bonn, 1962. See also J. Peterson, "Petri Nets," *ACM Computing Surveys,* Vol. 9, No. 3 (September 1977), pp. 223-52.

[4]   E. Yourdon and L.L. Constantine, *Structured Design: Fundamentals of a Discipline of Computer Program and Systems Design,* 2nd ed. (Englewood Cliffs, N.J.: Prentice-Hall, 1979). (1979 edition of Yourdon Press's 1975 text.)

18

THE FIRST PASTIST PRONOUNCEMENT

The Pastist Pronouncements were my fairly grouchy response to the great vogue of futurism that seized us toward the end of the 1980s. There were futurists everywhere—James Martin, Ed Yourdon, John Naisbitt, et al.—ordinary humans who professed to be able to see into the future and tell us what was going to happen next.

I personally always wanted to be a futurist, but when I peered into the future, I couldn't see squat. So I had to settle for being a "pastist."

Eventually, there were three Pastist Pronouncements. This one was about the great debate between people who loved the PC and its clones and those who loved the Mac (and thought the PC lovers had suffered permanent brain damage from doing too much DOS). It was written pre-Windows and so focused on OS/2, the then-great-hope of the PC community.

18

THE FIRST PASTIST PRONOUNCEMENT

First of all, a word about our friends, the futurists: For all their pronouncements, they manage not to have called (or even alluded to) the major developments of the last decade. Nobody forecast the advent of the VisiCalc phenomenon or of spreadsheets in general. There wasn't a word from the futurists about CASE. I saw Jim Martin's show in 1979, and he managed to forecast lots of things (the demise of rotating memory, for example, or the SNA revolution), but not the huge growth of the microprocessor industry. I think the PC and its impact took Martin and IBM by surprise, along with everyone else. Nobody forecast the workstation phenomenon.

Of course, futurists are entertainers, sustained by the amusement value, not the accuracy, of their forecasts. Nobody can see into the future. It's hard enough even to look back over the past and comment cogently on what has happened. Hard but useful. A person who provides this valuable service might be called a *pastist*. I humbly offer myself as a pastist until some real pro comes along. The pastist helps to make a more rational present by pointing out that something significant has occurred in the past, something that often only becomes apparent years later.

My initial pastist pronouncement risks being way off base. (No wonder forecasting the future is so hard if it's even hard to backcast the past.) But I offer it for what it's worth.

I am beginning to reinterpret the Apple Macintosh phenomenon as something far more significant than I had originally thought. My first view of it was that the Mac and its ilk were signs of important progress in the small computer field, progress that left the IBM offerings a good two years behind. That wasn't earthshaking, because IBM had always been a few years behind in everything. Like very savvy milers, they've known that the race belongs to the runner who holds a strong second place over most of the course. Their philosophy has been to let others lead the way, while they followed a mite more slowly but with great strength. This formula has done them proud for most of my lifetime.

Now something has changed. It's not just that IBM is behind the leader, but that they have not managed to maintain their position of being only two years behind. Let me put this in outrageously simplistic terms: If and when IBM manages to deliver a working OS/2, then I think they will be a full ten years behind the Mac. There are three things that lead me to this conclusion:

1. THE MODEST AMBITIONS OF OS/2

OS/2 seems to me to be relevant only for its fixes to problems of the PC/MS-DOS® world, problems that seem rather arcane to Mac users. During one of our recent company meetings, two Guild members spent a few sessions bringing the rest of us up to speed on why the PC was an important phenomenon (mostly because it was an emerging standard, and all the best efforts in new packaged software were focused on it). As a side effect, they had to expose us to some of the underside of living with the PC: a 1950s style memory management scheme, baroque and often awful video standards, a total anarchy of human interface approaches, an operating system that was little more than CPM in drag. One of them gave us a list of a few dozen utilities downloaded from CompuServe® that he found invaluable for dealing with his disks and managing his memory. The rest of us, mostly Mac users, compared notes on these utilities and concluded that there wasn't one of them that solved a problem that even existed on the Mac. They were part and parcel of the strange world of PC/MS-DOS.

Now along comes OS/2 (someday). Fanfare of trumpets and then the pitch: "Listen up thar' folks, here is a new system that actually makes it possible to use that little patch of memory between 512K and 635K that all you PC users paid for but could never figure out how to use! And that's not all!" Then comes the list of arbitrary and crazy restrictions that have plagued the PC world all these years that will be replaced by other arbitrary and crazy restrictions of OS/2. You get back the little slice of memory and you're not exactly limited to memory pages the way you used to be, but now you have to learn about the hard-coded 32-megabyte restriction on hard disk, about Setcom40 and its use to allow the operating system to see the serial port, about alt-esc and ctrl-esc cycling, 75 new rules for making a CON-FIG.SYS file with odd commands like MEMMAN=SWAP,MOVE and PRIORITY=DYNAMIC and DEVINFO=SCR, VGA,C:.DCP (something about CONFIG.SYS files strikes us Mac users as downright funny), about the 50+ special files that OS/2 needs to run at all, about DLLs, and more. Then, you get to learn about the positively bizarre charms of protected mode. Oh yes, there are some spiffy new utilities like PATCH, "a dual-mode command which lets you apply IBM-supplied corrections to fix faulty code" [1].

It's no secret that IBM is having a lot of trouble delivering OS/2 at all. But if they do, the kindest response that is likely to be offered by the Mac community after reflection on the great new offering is, "How quaint!"

2. THE CONSISTENCY AND STAYING POWER OF THE MAC DESKTOP

The Mac desktop and associated application conventions are a compelling and elegant framework for workstation use. I no longer look at the instruction book for anything. Programs all work alike, and they work in a way that makes intrinsic sense. When you suspect the existence of a feature, it shows up right where you first look for it. Things that ought to be built in are built in. Mouse conventions become second nature. You no sooner think "It would be nice if . . ." than you find just that, already built in. You uncover the richness at your own pace, working along fine with whatever your present level of sophistication is.

The strength comes from a kind of *integrity* that is present at all levels. One example: When a company called Matrix first came out with an expanded screen for the Mac, they plugged it in, made a simple change to the video ROM, and, by god, virtually every single program came up and ran perfectly on the larger screen, making full use of its size without ever explaining to any of the applications that something had changed. Then the Matrix people realized that buyers of their large screen still had a leftover small screen, so why not split the image over the two screens? They did that and, again, it came up without a whimper: Applications that had never considered the possibility of a larger screen, much less an image split over different screens with different pixel shapes and different aspect ratios, worked perfectly. You can drag icons from one screen to another, you never lose them in the cracks, you never get a window that can't be closed because its control parts are off screen . . . everything works.

Now, you might say that Apple just "lucked out" in that the multiple-screen fix turned out so easy. But can you ever imagine OS/2 "lucking out" on something like that? If you asked the OS/2 people to add a provision for multiple screen-mapping, they would come back to you with a delivery schedule and budget like that for Star Wars.

3. INVESTMENT

Apple's original investment in the desktop was $35 million. Part of that was a payment to Xerox for work that Xerox PARC had conducted earlier at even higher cost. There has been a huge investment since. The entire desktop is probably a $75 million item. Now here is the surprising thing about that amount: It's not all coding and debugging cost. The majority of that amount is pure think cost. I see no evidence that IBM is ready to make that kind of investment. They seem not to have invested much think cost at all in OS/2. Whatever the system cost them to build has been spent largely on coding and debugging and patching and documenting patches and testing the patches and incorporating a few features directly out of OS/360 JCL.

Well, there it is, the First Pastist Pronouncement: Apple has stolen a ten-year march on IBM. Of course, that has not been translated directly into revenue; the PC and its clones still predominate. But if I'm right, it does imply something about what has to happen next for PCs to remain competitive: IBM and Microsoft and the rest of the PC world are going to have a lot of catching up to do.

REFERENCE

[1] *Byte,* June 1988, p. 148.

19

THE SECOND PASTIST PRONOUNCEMENT

This Second Pastist Pronouncement is on the subject of software language. Although nothing much of note happened in this area during the 1970s and 1980s, feeling ran high nonetheless. In another essay, now lost, I observed that the end of the world cataclysm, if it comes, is not likely to be the result of any of the grand political causes that currently divide us. Rather, it will result from unresolvable conflict between the advocates of one computing language and another. Programmers feel strongly about their languages. There is no shortage of passion about the relative values of various languages. There is, however, a shortage of evidence.

19

THE SECOND PASTIST PRONOUNCEMENT

The languages we write our programs in have always been a subject for intense discussion and speculation; I can think of no other matter within our field able to generate so much emotion. I am emotional myself on the subject. Sometimes, I wake up in a pure red rage that Fortran and COBOL are still around, still muddying up what would otherwise be a rather elegant little world of Modula-2 and Oberon and SmallTalk. This rage has, on occasion, managed to cloud my normally sober judgment. For instance, there was that terrible day at the 1970 Spring Joint Computer Conference when I participated in a New Directions panel and predicted confidently that "COBOL will not survive the 1970s." (You can see why I renounced any career as a futurist.) In spite of the great *sincerity* of my utterance, COBOL perked along happily on its own agenda through the 1970s and 1980s, and, who knows, perhaps forever.

The period between 1970 to the present, then the exclusive domain of futurists, is now laid out behind us for careful consideration by the world's only announced pastist. "What happened in the field of computing languages during this period?" I ask myself. The answer is clear: Nothing.

That is not to say there weren't some wonderful possibilities dangled in front of the industry's nose. The third-generation languages—Modula, Simula, and Ada, for example—represent some of the finest work ever done in computing. Those whose names are linked to their development are among the most admired thinkers in our field: Ole-Johan Dahl, C.A.R. Hoare, Jean Ichbiah, Kristen Nygaard, and Niklaus Wirth. They are my personal heroes. They had some wonderful new languages to propose to us . . . but nobody went for them. You and I did, but we are statistical nobodies. The great body of our fellow practitioners slogged on as though the third generation never happened.

The third generation was largely a failure. Today, we live in a world of second-generation languages: COBOL, Fortran, and their derivatives (chiefly BASIC). The vitality of Fortran is particularly galling: It is as much a standard in the scientific community today as it was in 1969. In my capacity as president of MODUS (the Modula-2 Users' Society), I have watched the scientific community's staunch rejection of Modula-2. "Oh, it's got some cute stuff," the scientific programmers would tell us in explaining their decision to stick with Fortran, "but, see, we've got these really huge arrays. . . ." They could not convince themselves or be convinced that any new language could be as real world as what they were used to. As to the exquisite modularization and encapsulation features Modula-2 offered, well, that was just "cute stuff."

As microcomputers began to make their move, it seemed at last to be the death knell for COBOL. There were no reasonable COBOLs forthcoming on the new tiny machines, so what could the commercial programmers do but switch? And switch they did . . . to BASIC. To BASIC! From a second-generation commercial language to another second-generation language, this one not even oriented toward what they're doing. If we ever commission a series of paintings for the Smithsonian of Great Moments in Computing, I propose the switch to BASIC be among the first. I can see it in all its glory: A huge painted tableau hanging in the Hall of Science showing a commercial programmer being visited by an allegorical figure representing BASIC; the programmer's face is radiant with the dawning comprehension that this is to be the language of the twenty-first century.

If the third generation was a failure, the fourth generation was a nonstarter. 4GLs are wonderful, but (again speaking statistically) they simply have not left the blocks. There is every reason to use them heavily, to exploit their delightfully simple approaches, but their use has not caught on. In a recent empirical study of methods and tools [1], we found that there was less than one-half of one percent use of all 4GLs combined. (That is, a given program specified today has odds of less than 0.005 of being coded in a 4GL.) We found that Fortran, COBOL, BASIC, and BAL still are the languages of choice for a solid majority (55 percent) of practitioners. For all the hullabaloo over the 4GLs in the mid-1980s, it is now clear that the domain of problems to which they might be applied is considerably narrower than we had hoped. That accounts for a part of the weak acceptance of the languages; the rest is due to an ornery I'd-rather-fight-than-switch attitude.

In an attempt to explain why he thought Modula-2 was going to be an important language, Niklaus Wirth put his finger on the reason that it ultimately wasn't, and the reason for the poor acceptance of the rest of the new-generation languages: "The best language is not the one that makes it easiest to write a routine, but the one that gives you the best way not to have to write it." Reuse is the key. A language that comes with an extensive library of reusable components, together with facilities to access and exploit them in a manageable way, will provide a powerful incentive to switch. Modula-2 includes the facilities you need to take optimum advantage of such a library, as does Ada; but neither one yet has a library that is worth much. The Modula-2 library contains some 30,000 procedures and functions, and it is virtually useless. (The Ada library, the so-called Ada Environment, contains zero components and is utterly useless.) Clearly, a reusable component set would have to be two orders of magnitude larger than the Modula-2 library in order to entice people to switch languages. That is not going to happen quickly.

To make matters worse, the component libraries being built by users are quickly filling up with duplicates of all the best routines. Even the standard Modula-2 components libraries supplied by Wirth's group in Zurich have got a lot of duplicates, perhaps a dozen modules, for example, giving the same string-handling functions with varying degrees of elegance. As I observe this useless proliferation, I am struck by how important dynamic binding and inheritance can be in a language. In SmallTalk, for example, components could be improved over time without the proliferation and without the wasted effort.

Suppose, then, that there were an objective language that finally began to catch on, at least with the minority of people in our industry who are willing to consider new languages. Suppose that minority began the gargantuan task of building components and spreading their use, the "Software-ICs" that Brad Cox writes about [2]. Suppose they eventually accumulated a meaningful set of such ICs. Suppose, in addition, that programmers doing various kinds of specialty development began to assemble specialty IC libraries and to make them available to their peers, libraries of financial programming ICs, rate calculation ICs, customer record ICs, database ICs, trajectory tracking ICs, probabilistic calculation ICs, and the like. And suppose, finally, that the language and all its components could offer you the likelihood of a 50 percent or better reuse factor, meaning that more than half of the modules you need for your next application are already written and available free from the IC libraries. With all that available, would people then begin to desert Fortran and COBOL?

I don't know. For that, you'll have to ask a futurist.

REFERENCES

[1]   T. DeMarco and T. Lister, "Software Development: State of the Art vs. State of the Practice," *Proceedings of the 11th International Conference on Software Engineering* (Pittsburgh: 1989). (Reprinted in this volume as Essay 10.)

[2]   B. Cox, *Object-Oriented Programming: An Evolutionary Approach* (Reading, Mass.: Addison-Wesley, 1986).

20

TWENTY YEARS OF SOFTWARE ENGINEERING: LOOKING FORWARD, LOOKING BACK

In this Third Pastist Pronouncement, I turn to the effect of the U.S. Justice Department's actions against the giants of the computer field. This brief history of earlier antitrust campaigns is particularly relevant today as we consider the case against Microsoft. Is the world going to be a better place if Microsoft receives the same treatment that IBM, Xerox, and AT&T received in the 1970s?

20

TWENTY YEARS OF SOFTWARE ENGINEERING: LOOKING FORWARD, LOOKING BACK

The task of looking back over a period of such tumultuous activity and making a cogent statement of what has happened is sufficiently challenging for this panelist; I shall make no attempt to look forward.

The last twenty years have marked a coming of age for the software world, and for the information industry in general. The growth and contagious enthusiasm of this period have been remarkable. Computing and software in the 1980s has had some of the frenetic excitement of the space industry in the 1960s, World War II in the 1940s, radio in the 1930s, or electricity in the 1920s. I cannot think of another field of endeavor that would have been more enticing during my lifetime.

What is tempting today is to look back over the phenomenal growth of the last two decades and try to explain it in terms of the causative actions we took during the formative years. This might lead to statements of this form: "But for the monumental contributions of such technologists as _____, it is doubtful that the success of the period would ever have happened at all." In the blank, you fill in the names of those you admire or, better still, the names of other panelists, while expecting those other panelists to dutifully place your name on their position statements. What this lacks in historical veracity, it makes up for in effective self-promotion.

As tempting as that may be, I find myself persuaded that the key decisions that governed progress in our industry were made from outside the industry. They were not technological at all;

rather they were political. And their major effect was not to enhance the growth of the field, but to restrict it drastically. I refer to the stupid and ill-considered American public policy to weaken the major participants in the industry through the use and threatened use of antitrust legislation.

In the climate of 1989, it is difficult to conceive of American political action whose intent and purpose was the methodical crippling of the most successful players in a major growth industry. But that is exactly what the antitrust vehicle was from the end of the Eisenhower administration through the Kennedy and Johnson eras and into the first few years of the Nixon period. The specific targets were the three giants of the information age: IBM, AT&T, and Xerox. Each of the three was seriously weakened by the assault. The result has been reduced investment in research. AT&T was obliged to contribute perhaps the greatest technological breakthrough of all time, the semiconductor, to the "public good," and thus never profited at all from its investment. Xerox was similarly obliged to contribute its copier technology and, with it, the healthy revenue stream that would have funded its grand scheme of the early 1970s for integrated information processing. IBM, too, was pressured to allow the unheard-of atrocity of allowing its competitors to clone its products.

The most important new technology of the 1980s came to us directly and indirectly from Xerox PARC, the residuary benefit of research funding set during the time of Xerox's prosperity. Today, Xerox is a relative nonparticipant in the computer industry, and so the investment in basic research has been and will continue to be curtailed. The organization that gave us the transistor, AT&T Bell Laboratories, has been crippled; it seems safe to say that the Labs will never again be funded for the deep levels of research that it conducted from the 1930s through the early 1970s. IBM must be painfully gun-shy of investing in hardware or software that will be ripped off with impunity by its competitors.

The best ideas and methods developed within the field have had, I believe, small effect compared to the public policy blunders imposed upon us from without.

21

ROCK AND ROLL AND COLA WAR

Have you ever made the same dumb mistake twice? Welcome to the real world. Have you ever made the same dumb mistake a hundred times in a row? Welcome to the world of software development.

The topic here is organizations that learn from their mistakes and, just as important, organizations that seem unable to learn.

21

ROCK AND ROLL AND COLA WAR

Not previously published.

In early 1906, the Spanish philosopher George Santayana gave birth to a great quote. It appeared that year in his essay, "Life of Reason." If he'd fathered a child that same year, the child would now be dead and buried or getting there, but the quote lives on. It promises to be Santayana's most enduring contribution. Imagine, an entire life of writing and philosophizing now almost lost in the dust of obscurity, but the name Santayana is immortalized by a single line: "Those who cannot remember the past are condemned to repeat it."

Santayana's dictum is more often given in a slightly variant form: "Those who have failed to learn the lesson of history are condemned to repeat it." This is the kind of line that can find its way into practically any politician's stump speech. The Oliver Norths of the world use it almost hourly in campaign season. It has all the makings of great rhetoric: It is memorable, ponderous, and deeply, deeply true. Best of all, it confers a nice aura of superiority to the speaker (presumably one who *does* remember the lesson of history) at the expense of unspecified others, including the speaker's political opponents.

The lesson of history, of course, is whatever the speaker is trying to impress upon us as the way for right-thinking people and nations to act. Typically, the line is used to make a case against accommodation in all its forms, that is, against slimmer defense budgets, and against curtailed wheeling and dealing in faraway places. Accommodation, we are told, is contrary to the lesson of history, specifically to the lesson that Chamberlain gave the world in Munich in September 1938, where accommodation practically caused the second World War.

But the lesson of history is not as simple as that. From Chamberlain's point of view, the lesson of history was the way the first World War began in a spirit of no accommodation at all. The French, Germans, and Russians all had mobilized early and noisily, and had pushed to the brink, each sure that the others would flinch. Knowing that war was unthinkable, each side rattled its sabers and waited for someone else to accommodate. No one did, and the war was on. The lesson of history learned from the outbreak of World War I is almost precisely the opposite to the lesson learned from the outbreak of World War II. (If History wants us to get it straight, she had better learn to be more consistent.)

The lesson of history, though often stated simplistically, is never simple, and we do end up repeating it again and again. Our own field of software development is a perfect example. We seem to be stuck in a giant loop, repeating the same dumb mistakes in one project after another. After all these years, we still can't estimate, we still can't believe that we can't estimate (so we trust the latest set of numbers, even though the last few hundred sets were proved unrealistic), we still can't specify, we still can't reuse much of anything we've built before, and we still can't deliver software for what consensus dictates is the "right" price or in the "right" elapsed time.

On one project after another, we excuse doing things in a way that everyone knows is wrong because "there isn't time to do it right." We code before design, we design before specification, we specify before understanding the requirements. Then, at the end, we have a Lessons Learned meeting, where we point out that we really shouldn't do any of those things. Lessons Learned sessions are all the same (I know, I attend a lot of them). The people and the organizations and the applications may be different, but the actual lessons learned are the same. People raise their hands and grumble, "We really shouldn't set schedules based entirely on what Marketing would like to see and without regard to how much work there is to do." Everyone nods sadly. Another lesson learned. Again. Am I the only one who ever wonders why we keep relearning lessons we thought we had learned years ago?

THE TRANCE STATE CONJECTURE

When you take a wrong turn, then realize it's a mistake and backtrack, an automatic learning process is invoked that helps you avoid the mistake in the future. The process is not infallible, though. If you don't travel the same route for a few years, you may well make the same mistake again, but probably only one more time. The reinforced learning process is powerful. The second backtracking is almost certainly accompanied by a good deal of your muttering, "What a dummie!"

If you travel the same route every day and every single day make the same mistake, taking exactly the same wrong turn, there is something else going on. It's not that you haven't learned, but rather that your learned response is being over-whelmed by some unconscious but dominating need. I suggest the need is unconscious, because if it were conscious, you would understand its role in your route choice and not think of the turn as a "mistake." You might see it as unwise or imprudent or hope-less, but it is not a simple error.

When your actions are driven by forces that you don't completely understand, you are by definition in a kind of trance. The forces that drive you are hidden rules.

The propensity of software organizations to make the same mistakes again and again leads me to believe that these organ-izations are in a trance. On a conscious level, they believe their decisions are governed by clearly articulated and widely known rules like

- Keep quality high.
- Leave time for unanticipated problems.

- Respond to user needs.
- Work hard.
- Keep promises.

But there are also hidden rules at work. These hidden rules work on us without our noticing. They are universal, or nearly so; though they are never stated, we all understand them. When a hidden rule is in conflict with one of our publicly stated rules, the hidden rule almost always wins out.

The task I've set myself in this essay is an impossible one: to reveal all the hidden rules so we can acknowledge their influence and deal with them sensibly. Of course, I can never figure out what all the hidden rules are (after all, they're hidden), and I can't expect to know what special hidden rules may be working on you. But I do see a few that seem to apply widely. In the following list, I predict, you'll find a number of them that are at work within your organization.

HIDDEN RULE #1: FALSE PRECISION OF ESTIMATES

Suppose your boss asks for an estimate of how long it will take the team you currently have assigned to the Platypus Project to get the design wrapped up. And suppose you respond, "From 13 to 68 days." What reaction would you expect?

Few upper managers in my experience would sit still for such imprecision. They expect much tighter tolerances on an estimate, *even though past estimating performance has shown such tight tolerances to be completely unjustified.*

Common sense requires that the tolerance applied to your next estimate be consistent with the accuracy of your past estimates. If you and your organization have a history of estimates that are from 10 percent pessimistic to 150 percent optimistic, then your subsequent estimates should be packaged with similar error bands around them. Common sense requires this, but here common sense is at odds with a hidden rule. The hidden rule is that managers are supposed to be able to estimate with great precision. They are not however obliged to estimate with great accuracy. In such an organization, you would do better to estimate 15 days and be off by a factor of 4 than to break the hidden rule with an estimate like "from 13 to 68 days."

How much precision does the hidden rule require? Work it out in your own case by considering how wide a tolerance your boss would let you apply. My gut-feel is that tolerances of ±10 percent are pretty generally accepted, but nothing greater. Since estimates are usually required when 1 percent or less of the work is complete, ±10 percent tolerances are unreasonable to ludicrous. Nobody's estimating history could justify such a narrow confidence band.

The first time you try to use past experience as a guide for setting tolerances on new estimates, you're bound to hear this objection: "But we can't make sensible business decisions with such wide unknowns." Your response ought to be, "Is fibbing going to help?"

HIDDEN RULE #2: POWER SHIFTING

Workers in other fields must complain, as we do, that there is always too much politics in their organizations. But software workers are indeed subject to an extra portion of politics, due to an effect that is seldom discussed. It has to do with subtle changes in the power structure that accompany installation of any new system. The rule is this:

> Any time a new system is installed or an old one changed substantially, somebody gains and somebody loses power.

Those who build the system and put it into place are acting as agents for this changed power structure.

The parties who stand to lose the most are often the very ones that the system builders have to interact with in order to understand system functionality. These power-losers know that they are essential to the success of the new system. As you might imagine, they are not reluctant to use their temporary strength to force change on the new system, change that will conserve some of their eroding power. Or if that is not possible, they may use their present position destructively to hurt the system-building process and to make it painful for the builders.

A particularly ugly kind of project is one that effects a corporate consolidation, gathering the reins of power from the outlying regions and pulling them into a head office. The injured parties are many and the consolidators are few (but highly placed). The stakes are high and emotions higher. Nobody escapes from such projects without some damage.

If you fail to recognize power shifting, the politics at work on your project will be incomprehensible to you . . . incomprehensible and potentially deadly. The trance conjecture tells us that no matter how obvious the power shifts are, you may not be able to see them easily. You need to take mechanical steps to force your eyes to see: Ask yourself, Who stands to gain power? Who stands to lose? And how much? What behaviors are encouraged by these potential gains and losses?

HIDDEN RULE #3: ANGER

At a cocktail party one evening, I got into a discussion with a perfect stranger about our two different lines of work. She was in advertising. When I told her I was in computing, she smiled pleasantly. "Oh, that must be wonderful," she said. "Imagine a kind of work where nobody's feelings ever get hurt!" She assumed that since there is a well-defined, deterministic machine at the center of what we do, there would be no possibility of ugly interaction.

Interaction with the computer itself probably can't injure our feelings. We may be frustrated by a race condition or a subtle bug, but it never makes us feel unloved. There is, however, another side to our work. We spend a lot more time interacting with people than with machines, and, as you know, these inter-actions can be as ugly as those in any other profession.

The worst interactions involve a lot of anger. When the anger comes down on you from above, it can be particularly upsetting. What's surprising is that anger is routinely used by some managers to effect business purposes. For example, he or she uses fury to spur the project toward on-time completion or reduced cost. The cause of the anger seems to lie outside of the manager's normal emotional domain. If you slept with that mana-ger's spouse, you could understand the resultant emotional out-burst, but for a missed schedule? Or a late milestone?

The hidden rule at work here is a complex one having to do with the acceptability of emotions. This rule dictates that some emotions are distinctly not okay. Included in this group are fear and sadness. Other emotions are okay, particularly anger. The rule causes us to substitute an acceptable emotion for an unacceptable one. In most cases, this means showing anger when we feel fear.

Anger in the workplace almost always replaces fear.* When a boss yells at a subordinate over a slip or a defect, the boss is scared. When he rages, it means he is terrified.

The rule that anger is okay but fear is not is built deep into the human firmware. There is probably no changing it. But that doesn't mean there is nothing you can do to curb abusive anger by managers. If everyone understands the fundamental workplace truth that

$$\text{Anger} = \text{Fear}$$

then abusive anger will become a thing of the past. Managers who scream in rage will only be proving to everyone that they are scared to death. Since fear is not okay, they will have to stifle it. That doesn't solve the underlying problem, but it might at least lessen the impact on powerless subordinates.

---

*I use male pronouns for the boss in this paragraph because the effect is a bit more recognizable in men.

HIDDEN RULE #4: REPLICATION

Perhaps our experience in software design inclines us to look for solutions to the larger set that includes an immediate problem. Such an approach usually makes good sense in design. In management, however, it is just as often a mistake. The broader the measure, the less likely it is to have a huge point impact. The more elegant solution is likely to be the one that works for one problem and one problem only. The solution is elegant because it has a near perfect match to the problem space.

Sadly, these near perfect matches violate another hidden rule: Only replicatable solutions are really respectable. When you come up with a great trick that works on your project only, you get no credit. Yes, you saved two months by driving the application with Excel spreadsheets (so you avoided having to write input editors, formatters, print functions, and so on), but that trick can't be used in general. The fact that you finished two months early is written off to blind luck. Your stock in the organization would have been higher if you had written a normal input processor, put a lot of highly visible effort into process improvement, and finished on time or only a little late.

Great managers recognize the value of non-replicatable solutions. They know that the developer who benefits regularly from luck is a better manager than the one who doesn't. Mediocre managers, on the other hand, are threatened by any approach that is too tightly tailored to a specific situation. To such a manager, the best work-eliminating trick you come up with will only look like a lazy avoidance of hard work.

HIDDEN RULE #5: FAT

A hidden rule about management is that managing people is not by itself enough to justify managers' salaries. In order to be secure from the next round of cost-cutting, managers must be doing something other than just being boss. Managers who spend all their time giving direction to their projects, motivating individuals, and helping teams to form are nothing but (shudder) overhead, pure fat to be trimmed the next time there is trimming to be done.

This attitude affects us in two different but equally deadly ways: First, it contributes to the erosion of management in our organizations, the flattening of hierarchies so that even junior managers may have as many as twenty people directly reporting to them. No one can manage twenty people; setting up an organization with such wide management scope is a denigration of the management function. It assures that no real management gets done.

The second way this hidden rule hurts us is that it entices managers to find other roles to occupy them, in order to justify themselves. They get involved with the technology, serving as the project's chief architect or its ultimate quality gate. They go out as support on sales calls or pitch in with new ideas about extending the client base or marketing new services. Again, the result is that people are left unmanaged.

As Barry Boehm asserts, "Poor management can increase software costs more rapidly than any other factor." [1] The core functions of hiring, directing, and motivating people are what give management this impact. If management is so important, shouldn't we let managers do it? We should, but we don't because the hidden rule says not to.

HIDDEN RULE #6: DENIAL

The final hidden rule has to do with how we handle bad news. It suggests that admitting even the smallest defeat is defeatism. The manager who says, "Look, we're not going to make the April cutover date; let's start planning now for how we can deliver in July," is viewed as a defeatist. He or she would be better off politically by saying, "June at all cost. We can do it!" even though time went on to prove that June was impossible. Better off, even though late recognition of the facts made July impossible as well.

The attitude that is being thrust upon us is called "can-do management," an attitude that is responsible for more debacles than all other causes together. The can-do mentality has the effect of stopping bad news from moving up a hierarchy. Upper management will never even know that June is a problem because the can-do manager's "We can do it!" is the only message that makes it to the upper levels.

Can-do thinking makes risk management impossible. Since acknowledging real risk is defeatism, the risk management function in a can-do organization is restricted to dealing with those smallish risks that can be mitigated by quick action. That means you confront all the risks except the ones that really matter.

Defeatism is the gloomy tendency to think only of defeat even though victory may well be possible. It is not defeatism to acknowledge a setback. The best organizations deal with setbacks, even major lost battles, all the time.

Can-do management seems to work well only as long as nothing goes wrong. But things do go wrong at some time in most endeavors. The can-do organization then stays the course, ignores the truth that is known at all the lower levels, and thus escalates what might have been a minor setback into a true disaster.

When hidden rules stay hidden, they can do immeasurable harm. They gull us into making the same mistakes over and over and over again. We may never be entirely free of their influence, but we can do better. By seeking hidden rules, naming them, and discussing them in the open, we can hope to deprive them of some of the power they have over us.

REFERENCE

[1]   B.W. Boehm, *Software Engineering Economics* (Englewood Cliffs, N.J.: Prentice-Hall, 1981), p. 486.

22

SOMETHING OF MYSELF

In 1986, I was honored to receive the Jean-Dominique Warnier Prize for "lifetime contribution to the field of information science." The biographical statement that begins on the following page was also distributed to the audience at the awards ceremony.

22

SOMETHING OF MYSELF

Not previously published.

There is something very sobering about sitting down to write a biographical sketch to go with an honor like the Warnier Prize. The details of your life are expected to provide some answer to the questions in the reader's mind: What was it, after all, that this fellow really accomplished? How come he gets to lord it over the rest of us? What did he ever do to deserve all the fuss?

It helps to have been born a long time ago (1940, in my case). Hanging around for years and years is a prerequisite to almost any kind of recognition. When you're young and doing your best work, your peers will seldom notice. If they do notice, it's because you've chosen some different approach. In that case, they patiently set you straight and urge you not to deviate again from the wisdom of accepted practice. But when you're old and gray-haired and have the look of one who's resting on his laurels, people begin to suspect you may have accomplished something along the way.

A second important point on the path to any success is to arrange your early years so that you work under wonderful managers. I say this facetiously because the only way you can arrange this is to be damn lucky. It was my great good fortune to work under nine of the best imaginable managers, remarkable men and women who were dedicated to the development of human potential.

Among the best managers I've known were the ones who guided me in my early years at AT&T's Bell Laboratories: Lee Toumenoksa, Johnny Johanesson, John Nowak, and Al Stockart. Each of them took me under his wing at one time or another and taught me the best and truest thing he could. I am forever after obliged.

As I moved on, I was lucky enough to work for Jerry Wiener (one of the inventors of the concept of time-sharing), Shelly Weinberg (now at S.R.I.), Sharon Weinberg (now president of the Codd and Date Consulting Group), Gerard Bauvin (now president of La Sligos, a Paris software think-tank), and Sven-Olov Reftmark (one of the directors of Swedish Philips).

Some time ago, a friend observed to me that there were two ways to rise in the world: "You can be a star," he said. "That's the hard way. Or you can hitch your wagon to a star—that's the easy way." As I look back over the star managers I hitched up with through my career, it's clear that I have taken the easy way as much as possible.

In addition to some of the grand personalities and good breaks that Fortune threw my way, there was a small glimmer of inspiration of my own that helped me along. I began to realize almost from the beginning that we software people weren't really in the computer business. We said we were, and we certainly acted like members of any other high-tech community. But the business of software building isn't really high-tech at all. It's most of all a business of *talking to each other and writing things down.* Those who were making major contributions to the field were more likely to be its best communicators than its best technicians. The particular stars whom I looked up to, the Johanessons and Bauvins and Reftmarks, were gifted and practiced communicators. They spoke eloquently and wrote clear, concise text. When they presented an idea, you sometimes agreed and sometimes disagreed, but you always understood what they had said. That rare capability was something I set out to build in myself.

The software developer who sees his role as principally technical is inclined to begrudge the time that communication takes. Spend an afternoon honing a single page of text or working up a five-minute presentation? Not likely. Communicating is viewed as an onerous adjunct to the real work. But for me, communicating was the real work. With this new perspective, I began to change my discipline of writing and oral presentation. A quick, facile writer in the 1960s, I gradually began to slow down, to concentrate more and more on the rewriting process. Today, I am so slow that it takes me nearly a thousand hours to write the portion of a book or article that the eventual reader will breeze through in one hour. This may not seem like great progress, but it has served me well.

Along with my change of discipline, I began to make a change of style, a little less declamatory and more toward the story form. This meant presenting an idea by telling its tale, moving away from the approach of the essayists and closer to that of narrative writers. One of those, W. Somerset Maugham, described himself this way [1]:

> I go back, through innumerable generations, to the teller of tales round the fire in the cavern that sheltered neolithic men. I have had some sort of story to tell and it has interested me to tell it.

That may seem like a modest statement, but it really isn't. Those who made great art of their writing, the likes of Fielding, Chaucer, Shakespeare, James, Austin, Twain, and Conrad, were all storytellers. The preeminence of storytellers hasn't only applied in literature. The greatest man of science of the modern age, Charles Darwin, was a natural storyteller. His "single hand that rolled back the tide of ignorance" did it with a pen. As you look through his *Diary of the Voyage of the H.M.S. Beagle* or *The Origin of Species* today, you're most of all struck by the marvelous tale that the man had to tell and how well he told it.

There is always a tale to tell when you're trying to put a new idea across. I don't mean the war stories, which often just get in the way. I mean the tale of the idea itself. It has a beginning, a tickler that gets the reader or listener involved. It has a middle, in which the basic themes are developed and tension is built. Finally, it has a climax, the moment when (if you've succeeded) there will be a sudden flash of understanding through your audience and an almost audible "Aha!"

At least once a year, at tax time, I struggle with the requirement of describing myself in a single word in the box marked OCCUPATION. Am I a programmer? analyst? engineer? author? lecturer? Since it's the IRS that will be reading it, I don't struggle so much over the accuracy of the label as its likely auditability. But at least on this page and for your eyes alone, I label myself as I have aspired to be:

Tom DeMarco, Storyteller

REFERENCE

[1]   W.S. Maugham, *The Summing Up* (Garden City, N.Y.: Doubleday & Co., 1946).

TRANSLATOR'S NOTE

Since the early 1960s, I have dedicated a substantial quantity of my time and energy to translating important works in computing and software that might otherwise never have found their way into English. I have translated seminal articles from Italian, from Farsi (there is one of each of these in the following pages), from Greek, Urdu, Hungarian, Coptic, and ancient Hebrew.*

What I have to show for all this effort is nothing but an endless stream of vitriolic carping. Each time one of my translations is published, my mailbox is full of whining complaints. So-called experts on the various languages have propped up my translations side by side with the originals and set out to find fault. They criticize my shoddy phrasing, my inadequate understanding of the past pluperfect subjunctive, my ignorance of diacritical marks, my word choice, my interpretation, and everything else. Some of the complaints are demeaning in the extreme: "What ever made you think yourself competent to translate Greek?" they scream, "Have you no shame, sir?" It's enough to make a fair-minded person puke.

Enough, I say. Enough of this abuse. It's true that I have only a mediocre command of French, that my Italian is execrable, and my Farsi worse. But so what? Let those who are

---

*Here I refer to Scroll QM4M, the only one of the Qumran Canon to deal explicitly with the theory of automata and computational complexity.

more competent than my fallible self in these languages take on some of the burden that I have for too long shouldered alone. Let them translate the damn things themselves.

The fact is that all those complainers haven't done diddly to help bring these indispensable articles into English. As of today, the mind-bending thoughts of a Bombero Jacopini, for example, or a Faro ben Al-Faroush would be utterly unknown to English-language readers but for me.

I appeal to you, Dear Reader. You be the judge. On the following pages are two works that have transformed our science, a transformation made possible only by my translations. There you will find Jacopini's historic "Pasta e Fagioli," and Al-Faroush's mighty treatise, "Existence Modeling." The first seems like nothing more than a simple recipe, but is in fact an elaborate allegory that has become the defining statement of cybernetics. And second . . . well, second, the immortal work of Al-Faroush can speak for itself.

Read them and decide. Then you can tell me, my friends: Could I have done wrong by daring to translate these essential works?

23

Pasta e Fagioli

by Bombero W. Jacopini
Lanciafiamme del Informatica, Vol. 18, No. 3 (Fall 1993).

2 cloves garlic
4 tablespoons green (cold-pressed) olive oil
1 pound white navy beans
1 bottle of beer
2 bouillon cubes or 1 tablespoon red barley miso
2 cups crushed green olives (pitted) with brine
1 dollop of sherry
1 carrot
1 large onion
1 pound fusilli or rotini

Go back to the day before yesterday. Rinse beans and put them into a large crockery bowl and cover amply with water. If your beans are as old as mine typically are, add ¼ teaspoon of baking soda. Allow to stand overnight. Pour out water and rinse again. Cover one more time with water and allow to stand until time to cook. Pour out water and rinse yet again before using.

Today again. Pour beans into a large saucepan and cover with water. Add the bottle of beer. Add bouillon cubes or miso. Cook over medium flame for ninety minutes. Add liquid if necessary.

Meanwhile, slice garlic finely and sauté in half the olive oil in the bottom of a two-quart casserole. Slice and dice a large onion and add along with remaining olive oil. Simmer until translucent. Add beans. Add crushed green olives and brine. Stir over medium flame until thoroughly mixed. Cover and simmer for one hour, stirring occasionally.

Add sherry and cook off alcohol. Shred carrot into sauce and stir. Prepare pasta medium al dente. Allow sauce to simmer lightly while pasta is cooking. When pasta is ready, drain and turn into large warmed bowl. (Do not rinse pasta.) Add sauce and consume immediately.

Serves one.

24

Existence Modeling

by Faro ben Al-Faroush
Proceedings of the First Iranian Conference on Computing and Science, Teheran, 1986.

First came *system modeling* (now old hat). Then we got *data modeling*. Soon these puny efforts were surpassed by *enterprise modeling*, in which an entire organization could be reduced to little boxes and arrows on a huge piece of paper. But even this was not the ultimate. I now believe that the culmination of all modeling experience is at hand: *Existence Modeling*. Since this important new discipline seems likely to have impact on all of existence, I thought it useful to set down here some of its fundamental concepts. I limit my presentation to the following elegant and concise set of numbered insights, the fundamental lemmas of Existence Modeling:

1. The entire universe is made up of basic existence units (BEUs). All BEUs share one important characteristic: They exist.

2. There are two categories of BEU: discrete and continuous. These can be thought of broadly as *things* and *stuff*.

3. Things are neatly divided into two classes: good and bad.

4. Stuff is also made up of good and bad. Bad stuff has these qualities: It is slimy, foul-smelling, costly, contagious, left-wing, etc.

5. In general, bad stuff exceeds good stuff, *but this need not be so* (trust me on this).

6. Existence Modeling clarifies and elucidates all of existence through the use of *rigorous terminology*. For example, BEUs with good qualities are called *nice*. The opposite of nice is *lousy*.

7. There is also data.

8. Data doesn't actually exist. In fact, data is a basic non-existence unit (BNU).

9. In spite of its nonexistence, data is nice. In fact, all BNUs are nice. Consider these examples:
    ✓ God
    ✓ easy money
    ✓ free lunch
    ✓ bright employees who never give you any lip

    As you can see, all of these are inherently nice. The niceness of all BNUs implies that BNUs are divided into one class. (This has not yet been formally proved.)

10. Some BEUs are nice, but most are lousy.

11. You can't control what you can't measure. We can't currently measure the average niceness of BEUs, so it's out of control. Niceness of BNUs, on the other hand, is a uniform 100 percent.

12. This being true, the transformation from BEU to BNU is itself a nice BEU. Using the notation of predicate calculus, this can be written:

    (BEU —> BNU) = Good Stuff!

This transformation, when applied to people, however, is lousy.

13. Transformation from BEU to BNU is equivalent to the Buddhist concept of reaching Nirvana. When the transformation goes awry, you risk ending up as a cockroach.

14. Transformation in the other direction (BNU —> BEU) is a BNU. In spite of this, people spend most of their time trying to make it happen.

15. Each BEU may be characterized by its *quality*. Businesses and governments all over the world are enormously concerned with quality. It is discussed in sober-minded forums just about everywhere. Most of those discussing it eventually come face-to-face with this fundamental truth:

Quality is nice . . . provided it doesn't cost anything.

This truth follows axiomatically from the fact that costliness is a characteristic of bad stuff (see lemma 4, above).

16. Free quality is a BNU. That's what makes it so nice.

17. The average quality of everything can and should be improved, beginning now. This will require a total budgetary allocation of $0.00. (Those who do not understand why this is true have not been paying attention.)

As you can see, all of the Laws of Existence Modeling are deeply true—and useful. While people and organizations have existed for many millenia, none of them is all that good at it. They need help. Those who are into existence in any way have a great deal to learn from Existence Modeling, and incur a certain debt of honor to the esteemed sage, my humble self, who has first stated these essential truths.

BIBLIOGRAPHY

Austin, R. "Theories of Measurement and Dysfunction in Organizations." Ph.D. Thesis, Carnegie Mellon University, 1994. Forthcoming publication of Dorset House Publishing, New York.

Boehm, B. *Software Engineering Economics.* Englewood Cliffs, N.J.: Prentice-Hall, 1981.

_____ , and P. Papaccio. "Understanding and Controlling Software Costs." *IEEE Transactions on Software Engineering,* Vol. 4, No. 10 (October 1988), pp. 1462-77. Reprinted in *Software State-of-the-Art: Selected Papers,* eds. T. DeMarco and T. Lister. New York: Dorset House Publishing, 1990, pp. 31-60.

Booch, G. *Software Engineering with Ada.* Menlo Park, Calif.: Benjamin Cummings Publishing Co., 1983.

Business Means Business About Education. The Business Roundtable. New York: June 1989.

Collier, B., P. Fearey, L. Johnson, and M. Warner. *AppleSoft Postmortem Process, Version 1.1.* Apple Computer. Cupertino, Calif.: April 1994.

Contracting for Computer Software Development—Serious Problems Require Management Attention to Avoid Wasting Additional Millions. U.S. General Accounting Office, FGMSD-80-4, November 9, 1979.

Cox, B. *Object-Oriented Programming: An Evolutionary Approach.* Reading, Mass.: Addison-Wesley, 1986.

Cusumano, M. *Japan's Software Factories: A Challenge to U.S. Management.* New York: Oxford University Press, 1991.

DeMarco, T. *Structured Analysis and System Specification.* Englewood Cliffs, N.J.: Prentice-Hall, 1978.

_____ . *Controlling Software Projects.* Englewood Cliffs, N.J.: Prentice-Hall, 1982.

_____ . "Computing in the Schools: Turning Down the Glitz." *Human Capital,* July 1990.

229

_____, and T. Lister. "Programmer Performance and the Effects of the Workplace." *Proceedings of the 8th International Conference on Software Engineering.* London: 1985, pp. 268-72.

_____. *Peopleware: Productive Projects and Teams.* New York: Dorset House Publishing, 1987.

_____. "Software Development: State of the Art vs. State of the Practice." *Proceedings of the 11th International Conference on Software Engineering.* Pittsburgh: 1989. (Reprinted in this volume as Essay 10.)

_____, eds. *Software State-of-the-Art: Selected Papers.* New York: Dorset House Publishing, 1990.

Drucker, P. *The New Realities.* New York: Harper & Row, 1989.

Dyer, M., R. Linger, and H. Mills. "Cleanroom Software Engineering." *IEEE Software,* September 1987, pp. 19-25.

Gause, D., and G. Weinberg. *Exploring Requirements: Quality Before Design.* New York: Dorset House Publishing, 1989.

Halstead, M. *Elements of Software Science.* New York: American Elsevier, 1977.

Hopcroft, J., and D. Krafft. "Toward Better Computer Science." *IEEE Spectrum,* Vol. 24, No. 12 (December 1987), pp. 58-60.

Johnson, J., and G. Swogger. "Resistance Continuum." Menninger Business Institute, private correspondence, 1992.

Jones, C. *Programming Productivity.* New York: McGraw-Hill, 1986.

_____. *Assessment and Control of Software Risks.* Englewood Cliffs, N.J.: Prentice-Hall, 1994.

Kidder, T. *The Soul of a New Machine.* Boston: Atlantic-Little, Brown Books, 1981.

_____. *Among Schoolchildren.* Boston: Houghton Mifflin, 1989.

Kind, P. "Software as a Force Multiplier." *CrossTalk, the Journal of Defense Software Engineering,* Vol. 7, No. 7 (July 1994), pp. 2-11.

Knuth, D. "Structured Programming with Go To Statements." *Current Trends in Programming Methodology,* ed. R. Yeh. Englewood Cliffs, N.J.: Prentice-Hall, 1977.

Lederer, A., and J. Prasad. "Nine Management Guidelines for Better Cost Estimating." *Communications of the ACM,* Vol. 35, No. 2 (February 1992), pp. 51-59.

"Lou Mazzucchelli on Software Engineering." *Computer Design,* August 1991, pp. 25-27.

Maugham, W. *The Summing Up.* Garden City, N.Y.: Doubleday & Co., 1946.

McCabe, T. "A Complexity Measure." *IEEE Transactions on Software Engineering,* Vol. SE-2, No. 12 (December 1976), pp. 308-20.

McCue, G. "IBM's Santa Teresa Laboratory—Architectural Design for Program Development." *IBM Systems Journal,* Vol. 17, No. 1 (1978), pp. 4-25. Reprinted in *Software State-of-the-Art: Selected Papers,* eds. T. DeMarco and T. Lister. New York: Dorset House Publishing, 1990, pp. 389-406.

Mills, H. "Top-Down Programming in Large Systems." *Debugging Techniques in Large Systems*, ed. R. Rustin. Englewood Cliffs, N.J.: Prentice-Hall, 1971.

Myers, G. *Reliable Software Through Composite Design.* New York: Petrocelli/Charter, 1975.

A Nation at Risk. U.S. Government Printing Office. Washington, D.C.: 1983.

Norman, D. *The Design of Everyday Things.* New York: Basic Books, 1988.

Parnas, D. "On the Criteria to Be Used in Decomposing Systems into Modules." *Communications of the ACM,* Vol. 15, No. 12 (December 1972), pp. 1053-58.

Peterson, J. "Petri Nets." *ACM Computing Surveys,* Vol. 9, No. 3 (September 1977), pp. 223-52.

Petri, C. "Kommunikation mit Automaten." Ph.D. Thesis, University of Bonn, 1962.

Ritti, R., and G. Funkhouser. *The Ropes to Skip and the Ropes to Know.* New York: John Wiley & Sons, 1987.

Robertson, J., and S. Robertson. *Complete Systems Analysis: The Workbook, the Textbook, the Answers.* New York: Dorset House Publishing, 1994.

Ross, D., and J. Brackett. "An Approach to Structured Analysis: An Analysis Technique Similar to Structured Programming Enables Systems to Be Designed More Effectively." *Computer Decisions,* Vol. 7, No. 9 (September 1976), pp. 40-44.

Roze, U. *The North American Porcupine.* Washington, D.C.: Smithsonian Institution Press, 1989.

Sciacca, P. *Retrospective: A Time for Reflection on Process Effectiveness at the Conclusion of Product Production and Delivery.* AT&T. Columbus, Ohio: February 1994.

Selby, R., V. Basili, and F. Baker. "Cleanroom Software Development: An Empirical Evaluation." *IEEE Transactions on Software Engineering,* Vol. SE-13, No. 9 (September 1987), pp. 1027-37. Reprinted in *Software State-of-the-Art: Selected Papers,* eds. T. DeMarco and T. Lister. New York: Dorset House Publishing, 1990, pp. 256-76.

Smith, P., and D. Reinertsen. *Developing Products in Half the Time.* New York: Van Nostrand Reinhold, 1991.

Stevens, W., G. Myers, and L. Constantine. "Structured Design." *IBM Systems Journal,* Vol. 13, No. 2 (May 1974).

Tajima, D., and T. Matsubara. "The Computer Software Industry in Japan." *IEEE Computer,* Vol. 14, No. 5 (May 1981). Reprinted in *Software State-of-the-Art: Selected Papers,* eds. T. DeMarco and T. Lister. New York: Dorset House Publishing, 1990, pp. 76-86.

Weinberg, G. *Quality Software Management, Vol. 1: Systems Thinking.* New York: Dorset House Publishing, 1992.

Yamaura, T. "Standing Naked in the Snow." *American Programmer,* January 1992.

Yourdon, E., and L. Constantine. *Structured Design: Fundamentals of a Discipline of Computer Program and Systems Design,* 2nd ed. Englewood Cliffs, N.J.: Prentice-Hall, 1979. (1979 edition of Yourdon Press's 1975 text.)

Zahn, C. "A Control Statement for Natural Top-Down Structured Programming." *Symposium on Programming Languages.* Paris: 1974.

INDEX